CHRISTIAN BEGINNINGS

CHRISTIAN BEGINNINGS

THREE LECTURES

BY

F. C. BURKITT, D.D.

NORRISIAN PROFESSOR OF DIVINITY
IN THE UNIVERSITY OF CAMBRIDGE

Eugene, Oregon

Wipf and Stock Publishers
199 W 8th Ave, Suite 3
Eugene, OR 97401

Christian Beginnings
Three Lectures
By Burkitt, F. Crawford
ISBN: 1-59752-459-X
Publication date 12/5/2005
Previously published by University of London Press, 1924

CHRISTIAN BEGINNINGS

LECTURE I

IN calling this set of lectures " Christian Beginnings " it must be obvious to everyone who is likely to take any interest in them that I had in view the work called *The Beginnings of Christianity*, now being edited by Professors Foakes Jackson and Kirsopp Lake, of which the first volume appeared in 1920 and the second in 1922. These two volumes, the work of many distinguished scholars besides the two professors who are the chief editors, deal with Prolegomena to the subject in general and to the Book of Acts in particular. Not all the writers are in harmony, or write from the same critical or religious standpoint. I myself contributed a chapter to the second volume, so that it is hardly proper for me to praise or blame the work in general terms, nor would a mere review be a suitable proceeding for lectures such as these. Nevertheless, I think that the topics treated of in Professors Jackson and Lake's undertaking do afford very proper matter for discussion here. The two volumes have raised very serious issues, both by the treatment of new questions and still more by the treatment of old questions in a fresh way, in the discussion of which I desire myself to offer some observations.

And first of all the general plan and treatment of *The Beginnings of Christianity* may serve to remind us how far we have moved in the last hundred years, not only in technical questions connected with the rise of Christianity, but in the general point of view. Disbelief in orthodox Christianity and in the official account of its claims and genesis is no new thing; it was no new thing a century ago. The age of Gibbon and of Porson was not an age of Faith. But there is a curious difference between the public attitude then and now towards the Gospel history and its sequel. Orthodoxy, or it would be really more accurate to say certain parts of orthodox theory, appeared to be then in possession ; to say certain things, to call in question certain views, was then to challenge authority, to give a shock to generally acknowledged conventions. The Mosaic authorship of the Pentateuch and the general correctness of the Mosaic chronology, the historicity of the Gospel narratives (with the possible exception of some of the miracles), and above all the practical agreement of the true apostolical teaching with that of the most enlightened views of the day,— these things were generally assumed. There was this difference, that the orthodox Protestant Nonconformist and the orthodox member of the Church of England differed somewhat in their own views and so regarded the true apostolic teaching somewhat differently ; but though they differed in their presentation of the views of the Apostles they were agreed that the Apostles were right. The " corruptions of Christianity " came later, according to this theory, and these went from bad to worse, until they ended in manifest Popery.

We have travelled a long way since those days. We have become more enlightened and tolerant, and have learned an evolutionary view of human thought and social organization. For the old orthodoxy, regarded as a fixed system, exists no longer. It is not merely that breaches have been made in the wall, or that projections which stood in the way of modern thought have been cleared away: the whole building has collapsed. Where Gibbon saw an effete and old-fashioned building, we are confronted with a heap of ruins. There are few stones one upon another that have not been thrown down; but the heap remains—what are we to make of it?

When I say that the old orthodoxy is dead, let me explain that I am not thinking so much of Religion itself as of the explanation of Religion, of the account which is given of what Christianity is and how it came to be there. A hundred years ago a fairly definite answer was generally ready to hand; now, though there are many Christians still, definite answers are not so readily forthcoming, and such answers as there are differ greatly from each other and from what was said in former centuries.

What I mean will perhaps be more clear to you if I remind you that a hundred years ago one favourite answer as to what Christianity is, was widely known as the Plan of Salvation. I am not going to describe the Plan of Salvation in detail, far less dissect it to an unsympathetic audience: notwithstanding all its crudities it is much too near to historic Christianity for that sort of treatment. But let me remind you that it describes the counsels of God Himself, that it assumes the predictions of the prophets of Israel, that it explains in a couple of sentences the inner meaning of the Nativity and of the Cross, and that it foresees the future of the human race. It was believed that the Plan of Salvation had been extracted from the Bible: in practice, the Bible was interpreted to agree with the Plan of Salvation. There were those a hundred years ago who did not like the formulation of this famous Plan, which for generations was supposed to be the theme of every Protestant sermon. But these others also had their fixed theological scheme, and almost always they interpreted the Bible on its lines. Christianity itself was not a problem: the only problems consisted in those parts of the Bible which seemed difficult to reconcile with the scheme.

Now all this is gone, or it has an influence only in very restricted circles. We look at the earliest Christianity, the data given us in the New Testament, as a *problem*, in a way that seems to me new. We are able, in fact we are compelled, to look at Christian Beginnings objectively as no previous generation of Christians, sincere or nominal, were ever able to look at them. With our evolutionary philosophy—perhaps some Catholics would prefer to say, with our ideas of Development—we are not obliged to find all our most cherished convictions, all the deepest expression of Religion, within the covers of the New Testament. We need not expect to find all true theology formulated somewhere by St. Peter, St. John, or St. Paul. We are at least more willing than former generations were to let the documents speak for themselves, because—let us squarely confess it—we are not quite so sure beforehand that the documents will speak the truth. We are still prejudiced—who is not?—

but at least we have dropped the prejudice that the Apostles, properly understood, must really have thought as we do.

The *Beginnings of Christianity*, planned on such a generous scale by Professor Jackson and Professor Lake, was designed to tell us what the Apostles and the rest of their contemporaries really meant and thought, without prejudice, or as little as might be. But the impression which the first volume made, at least in this country, was rather unfavourable. I think this unfavourable impression is itself worthy of some consideration. It takes two to make an impression; that which impresses and that which is impressed. It was not only what the editors said: it was partly the sentiment, I will not say the prejudice, of the readers. The sentiment I mean is current among a large number of more or less "liberal" Christians in England, who on the one hand are repelled by the rigidity of the old dogmatic definitions and formulas, but on the other, have not acquired correspondingly clear ideas and expressions to take their place.

Such persons often make up for the instability of their beliefs about "God" and "Christ" by an honorific reverence in language and expression. They like to praise and admire Jesus rather than to try to understand Him, so that they were repelled by the careful wording of *Beginnings*, i 285–294, in which an attempt is made in the clearest language to characterize the actual teaching of Jesus and the nature of the authority which He claimed. It sounded to many cold and inadequate. And when it was found that later on in the volume the editors, together with their learned collaborator, Professor George Foot Moore, were inclined to doubt whether Jesus claimed for Himself the titles of "Messiah," "Lord," and even "Son of Man," many readers were—to use the New Testament word—scandalized.

It is curious how much more anxious Christians always have been to say "Lord, Lord," in the right tones than to do the things that Jesus said. But it is also easy for the curious observer to be cheaply cynical on the subject, and I only touch upon the point here at the outset to remind myself as well as you of the immense importance that what may be called Loyalty to Jesus holds in the effective formulation of the Christian Religion. What Professors Jackson and Lake said in the section I have just referred to was in reality quite orthodox ; it was an attempt to describe clearly in unconventional words what the Gospels tell us. I venture to think that what a good many disliked in it was that it did not *sound* loyal enough, for it was not expressed in the usual tones of panegyric, and therefore it seemed to be inadequate.

As I said just now it is not my design to make a review of this book, but if I take certain points connected with the beginnings of Christianity, in the order adopted by Jackson and Lake, and start from their presentation of the points, I shall only be following the natural and almost inevitable order. Beginning, therefore, after very good precedents, with the Baptism of John, I meet on p. 103 with the phrase "According to Mark and Q the mission of John was fundamentally eschatological." This of course is what is generally said, or something like it, but I venture to think it is misleading. That what are called eschatological views were very widely spread and very earnestly held among the Jews of St. John's day is most certainly true. In my opinion these beliefs were one of the chief factors in the Jewish history of the period, beliefs so widely and so earnestly held that they led the nation some 30 or 40 years later to the desperate and disastrous rebellion against Rome. But, as I read the evidence, John the Baptist did nothing to foster these views. In common with his countrymen he thought, no doubt, that the End was near, but I do not think he thought it was any nearer than others thought it, or that he thought it his business to remind his hearers of the nearness of the End.

Especially is this clear if we take our authorities to be, as Jackson and Lake rightly do, Mark and Q. Mark tells us that John set forth a practice of baptism for the remission of sins, but the only teaching about the future that he mentions is that John did not regard himself as the last stage:

someone greater than he would come after and baptize with holy spirit. As for Q, that has to be distilled out of Matthew and Luke. The fullest account of what John used to say is given by Luke and is chiefly remarkable for rough practical ethics: be kind to those worse off than yourselves, don't cheat, don't bully. That the End is near is assumed as common ground between *NB* the Hermit and those who have come out to him, but it is not the subject of his talk.

The same is true of what we find in Matthew, except for a single phrase, but it is the first phrase given, and (as our Bibles are bound up) it is the first sentence about John in the New Testament—" In those days came John the Baptist, preaching in the wilderness of Judea, and saying, Repent ye : for the kingdom of heaven is at hand " (Matt. iii 1, 2). This sentence has dominated too much both popular and learned notions about John. It is just one of those cases where the literary analysis of the Gospels, which has been so minutely carried out in the past two generations, can really guide us to a better appreciation of the historical figures they depict, for the "Matthaean" phraseology that this passage contains itself suggests to us that the details in which it differs from the parallel in Luke may be regarded as the Evangelist's manner of telling the story rather than as fresh historical information.[1] Nothing is more characteristic of Matthew's style than his fondness for repeating his own phrases; here the message of John and the message of Jesus in Matt. iv 17 have been assimilated. "The Kingdom is at hand" is indeed the message of Jesus (Mark i 15; Luke iv 43, xvi 16), but the message of John was comprised in the single word "Repent!"

The "message" of John, the "preaching" of John,—I am not sure that either of these words is quite appropriate. According both to the Gospels and to Josephus, John's "advice" would seem a more correct description. Whatever the degree of his prophetic inspiration he did not go out of his

[1] Not only "Kingdom of Heaven" for "Kingdom of God," but also the use of παραγίνεται is exactly in the manner of Matt. ii 1, iii 13. And further, the sentence is immediately followed by one of the characteristically Matthaean formulas to introduce a prophecy.

way to warn his contemporaries. On the contrary, he remained in far-away solitudes, and we do not know at all how he became a public character. However, he did so and acquired the fame that attaches in the East to the Holy Man. He seems to have attracted some more or less regular disciples, who followed his personal fortunes, but the main sphere of his influence was upon persons who went out into the wilderness to see him and then returned to their homes. To these he gave good advice as to how they should behave so as to please God ; no doubt in some cases it was followed, and many more would always reverence the memory of the inspired sage. But it does not appear that he founded a permanent sect or school, or that all those who had been " baptized " in his presence called themselves Disciples of John.[1]

[1] The Fourth Gospel represents John as surrounded by a band of disciples, but even here it is not said that these disciples themselves baptized and so carried on the tradition to others. The personal followers of John are said in Matt. xiv 12 to have come to Jesus after John's execution, but the corresponding passage of Mark makes it appear that this is rather a deduction of the Evangelist than a piece of independent tradition. It is from Mark ii 18 and Acts xix 3 that the existence of what might be called a Johannine *sect* has been inferred. But Mark

As Jackson and Lake point out (p. 102), it is not quite clear what significance was attached by John to the rite of baptism, so inseparably connected with his name. That is to say, it is not clear from the account in Josephus whether the dipping in water was originally recommended to those who had only lately become conscious of sins and were therefore at the beginning of a new manner of life, or was for those who were already "ascetics," already making an especial practice of virtue. In another passage (*Beginnings*, p. 334), it is pointed out that the word βαπτίζειν in pre-Christian times is rather rare, being used only four times

---

ii 18 does not really imply a separate sect; it means no more than that those who had gone out to John, and under his influence had determined to amend their lives, observed as strict a rule as the Pharisees. Acts xix 3 again, a story about some Ephesian Jews in A.D. 51, only tells us that some Jews in the provinces, who had come under John's influence twenty years before, still retained a vivid memory of his teaching and were living more or less in accordance with his precepts. Even if the story as told by the Christian Evangelist is accurate in detail it does not imply a succession of Johannites forming a kind of rival sect to the Nazarenes. Nothing is said that points to these Ephesians having been an organized community, which one entered, or was initiated into, by a rite of "Johannine" baptism administered elsewhere than in the River Jordan.

in the Septuagint, yet John is called ὁ βαπτισ-
τησ both by Josephus and in Christian
tradition. The deduction I should draw
is not that "the word was coming into use
in Greek-speaking Jewish circles," but that
it was in some way brought into use through
the practice of John himself. In this
connexion it is important to remember that
John had retired to the Jordan, and that it
was in the Jordan water that his penitents
bathed. In other words he told them to do
what Naaman did of old, and the cleansing
bath of Naaman in Jordan is one of the four
places where βαπτίζειν occurs in the Greek
Bible.[1] We are taught to regard John as
Elijah, but as the Baptist he rather corresponds to Elisha.

What, then, did people go out into the
wilderness for to see? As I said just now,
the message of John may be condensed into
the single word " Repent ! " But this word
is more complicated than it sounds to us now
after so many Christian centuries. What
did it mean to those who heard John?
What word did John himself use? The

[1] 4 Regn. v 14, ἐβαπτίσατο.

Greek is μετανοεῖτε, the Aramaic is *tūbhu*, i.e. "return." What do these words really imply?

We Christians expect to hear from religious teachers exhortations to "repentance." We expect them to tell their hearers to change their opinions and their mode of life, and this is called "repentance." But the word "repentance" does not occur in a number of religious writings where we might have expected to find it. There is no μετάνοια, no "repentance," in the Greek Psalter, nor is "repentance" a leading term of St. Paul's religion.[1] And if John the Baptist, as we must suppose, spoke in Aramaic and what he said was "Turn round!" "Return!" what did he mean by that? Mark's phrase for the religion of John is "a baptism of repentance for remission of sins"—what is implied? I am afraid that we tend to understand this phrase by the analogy of the Creed, and to treat it as if it said "baptism for remission of sins," without mentioning the repentance. But this interpretation puts the emphasis on the

[1] See 2 Cor. vii 9, 10.

wrong word if, as I believe, Luke iii 7–14 gives a good idea of John's teaching. I think Mark is telling us that John taught that remission of sins was to be obtained by turning round to a new and better way of life, a new start which was symbolized and confirmed by washing in the Jordan, like Naaman, who (as we are told) promised the Prophet that henceforth he would worship no other God save the LORD only. Neither pride of birth nor worldly position would avail with God, nothing but an amended life, yet one practicable for every class in the station in which they happened to be.

As I understand it, the teaching of John was wholly ethical. A good life henceforth (said he in effect) may save a man in the coming visitation of God, and nothing else will. But besides the homely, straightforward advice there must have been the personal influence of the Prophet. It must have been great : we have the testimony of Jesus to it. " No one born of women greater than John the Baptist "—what sort of a personality must that have been which called forth this great encomium? Besides this there are inferences to be drawn from the tale of the Baptism of Jesus. It is a commonplace of commentators that the story of the Temptation, if historical, must have come from Jesus Himself, for there was no other witness. But the same may be said of the story of the Baptism. It is hardly fair to call in the Fourth Gospel and refer the story to the Baptist, for according to the Fourth Gospel the descent of the Spirit takes the place of the Baptism altogether.[1] It seems to me far more likely that the story of the Baptism in Mark is something which Peter remembered of what his Master had once told him, and that it testifies to the overwhelming impression that intercourse with the Baptist had made upon Jesus. It was what we now glibly call "religious experience"; it revealed our Lord to Himself, and it sent Him into the wilds to think out what course He was intended to take.

I do not propose to discuss here the Gospel history; our subject is the beginnings of the Christian Society and the problems

[1] John i 32–34.

confronted by it. But this seems a convenient place to consider some of the various titles by which Christians spoke of Jesus, or that were used by Jesus Himself. We have just had the story of the Temptation in our minds ; let us begin with that. The story occurs in Matthew and Luke and may reasonably be referred to what is called Q, though of course to label a story or a saying " Q " really tells us no more than that we have evidence that the story or the saying was current in a more or less fixed form before " Matthew " and " Luke " wrote. Well, the story, if historical, must be something told by Jesus to His disciples, something therefore intended to reveal His thoughts, His own state of mind, at the outset of His career. " If Thou be Son of God," says the tempter to Jesus : " Thou art My Son," the Voice had said to Him at the Baptism. This title, then, " Son of God," υἱὸσ θεοῦ, comes first in time and thought according to the tradition. What, or rather, how much, does it imply ?

We can best answer this by considering the sequel. It seems to me that it is unsatisfactory to equate the three temptations with (1) the use of miraculous powers for bodily satisfaction, (2) the use of miraculous powers for display, (3) the pursuit of worldly glory. As Matthew Arnold once said of another matter, " It is to consider too curiously to consider so." The temptations are far more vague, more intangible, more internal. For my part I am quite ready to believe that they represent the impressions that Jesus retained of His time of solitude, clothed in the language that came natural to Him. They are not an artificial parable of anything. And what was the result ? The result was purely negative. Satan leaves Him for a season and angels minister to Him, but the course of action He was to pursue was no clearer than before. The call came from outside, from the course of events. It was when John's activity was cut short, when Herod had arrested the Prophet of practical ethics, that Jesus hears the inward call to act, and comes with a message to Galilee (Mark i 14, followed in Matt. iv 12).

And just as I consider the three temptations to be reminiscences of interior struggles with half-defined tendencies, vague, yet vivid, rather than the rejection of three clearly realised courses of action, so also with the title " Son of God." Vague yet vivid— I think this phrase also suits the manner in which this title is used in the story of the Temptation. I seem to see in this story Jesus become conscious of internal power, conscious that He is not altogether like His friends and acquaintance, conscious that the familiar phrases of worship and religious metaphor mean, or have come to mean, something real and special to Himself. He had said " Our Father " in the synagogue, Sabbath after Sabbath, with the rest of the worshippers;[1] but to Him this name had come to be something more intimate and individual. To what end? What was He meant to accomplish?

I have begun with " Son of God " rather than with " Messiah " or any other of the Christological titles, because I believe it to be really more primitive. Later on the term became a watchword of theologians,

---

[1] See the Eighteen Benedictions (both recensions), and the *Kaddish*.

but as used in the story of the Temptation it seems to me mainly personal. In discussing the terms by which Christians spoke of their Lord we move for the most part among theological ideas, notions of divine rank and dignity. It is all the more striking that the sacred tradition tells us that the first effect upon Jesus of a consciousness of special relation to God was neither exaltation nor timidity, but an earnest consideration of what He ought to do.[1]

Ever since 1901, when the epoch-marking book of Wrede upon the Secret Messiahship in the Gospels appeared, there has been a controversy how far Jesus regarded Himself as "the Messiah" or "Christ," or allowed Himself to be so regarded. But the paragraphs by Professor G. F. Moore on early Jewish ideas about Messiah (*Beginnings*, vol. i, pp. 346-362) show the English reader that we have not merely to consider whether

---

[1] With reference to the significance of the phrase "Son of God" in the story of the Temptation and its psychological priority to other titles, I should like to refer to a review by Dr. Bethune Baker in the *Hibbert Journal*, xiv 830 (for 1915-16).

Jesus is properly to be regarded as " the Jewish Messiah." Christians have been too apt in the past to assume that there already existed among the Jews a fairly definite and uniform conception of the Messiah who was expected to come. That indeed is a notion presupposed in many Christian documents, particularly in the Fourth Gospel (e.g. John i 41, 49 ; iv 25f ; x 24), but it is not borne out by a study of Jewish literature. Not all pre-Christian Jewish anticipations of the End included the figure of a Messiah or solemnly consecrated Vicegerent of God, and when such a figure does appear, his rôle and person were conceived in the most diverse fashion. The old idea that the Jewish expectation was essentially the expectation of a Messiah, that the conscious hope of every Jewish girl was that she might turn out to be the destined mother of the Messiah —these presentations have little foundation in fact. If true at any time of the Jews it was of the mediaeval Jews living in Christendom, with beliefs partly shaped by reaction from Christian beliefs. Sabbatai Ṣevi in the 17th century believed himself to be the true Jewish Messiah, as distinct from the Christians' Messiah : he was but the last and most notable of a whole series of pretenders, beginning with Bar Cochba in A.D. 135. But before Bar Cochba, we do not read of any Jew who gave himself out to be the Messiah.

All this is generally recognized by scholars acquainted with Jewish literature, but its importance is not even yet sufficiently gauged by students of the Gospel and of Christian beginnings. I believe in the historicity of St. Peter's confession near Caesarea Philippi, but it seems to me that Christians too much regard that confession as the guessing of a riddle. It has been supposed that the veil had only to be torn from Peter's eyes to enable him to recognize in his Master the familiar features of the longed-for Christ. But if the Christ to the pre-Christian Jew was what Professor Moore shows us, a figure diverse in conception and rather shadowy in outline, then Peter's confession was more than the correct solution of an already worked-out problem : it was a synthesis, an Act of Faith indeed, for it was a giving of substance to something that had never been seen before. The name and title is not refused by Jesus, at least within the inner circle of disciples, but the chapters of Mark which follow are meaningless, unless the certainty of coming trial and disaster was more vividly present in His mind than any ultimate glorification.

What I seem to read from the documents, what is emphasized in Mark as uppermost in the mind of Jesus, is not the choice of this or that epithet or title as the most appropriate, but the irresistible sense of vocation. And this took shape in a conviction that the God of Israel, who had called Him Son in a special sense not shared by others, had marked Him out thereby as the instrument of bringing in (or at least hastening) the End of the present state of things by His becoming in some way a sacrifice or ransom for the elect. In Mark x 45, this is condensed into a single saying, but it is implied everywhere.

As I said, I do not intend to review the Gospel history, but it is fitting here to consider briefly the two conceptions of Jesus as the Son of Man and as the Suffering Servant. The discussion of the title Son of

Man in *Beginnings*, vol. i, 362ff, seems to me to supersede all that is available in English previously written. No doubt it is not the last word on the subject, but it cannot be ignored.

The study of Jewish Apocalyptic literature, particularly of Enoch and of 4 Ezra, has revealed to the last generation what is implied by the title " Son of Man," ὁ υἱὸσ τοῦ ἀνθρώπου, so common in the Gospels, so rare in the rest of early Christian literature. "This is He who has been appointed by God as judge of the living and the dead " (Acts x 42), God "will judge the world in righteousness by that man whom He hath ordained " (Acts xvii 31),—these familiar verses from the Book of Acts give an excellent description of the office and person of the Son of Man, and the Gospels represent Jesus speaking of this Son of Man in such a way that it is clear that He means Himself. So far from being a term of humiliation it is a high and supernatural honour.

But further consideration of the term brings in a host of difficulties and obscurities, some of them linguistic, some literary and critical. The Greek words ὁ υἱὸσ τοῦ ἀνθρώπου make up a phrase which if unidiomatic and bizarre is at least definite. The readers of the Gospels in Greek no doubt felt as we do in reading the English version. We feel that we are dealing with a technical term, a translation of some phrase that was perspicuous in the original language from which it has been adapted. But when we go back to the original language, in this case Aramaic, we find that it is only a literal rendering of the regular Aramaic term for "man," an individual of the human race. So far as any verse in the Gospels is a literal rendering of an original Aramaic sentence there is no linguistic reason why every time ὁ υἱὸσ τοῦ ἀνθρώπου occurs it should not have been rendered simply by ὁ ἄνθρωποσ or why every time ὁ ἄνθρωποσ occurs it should not have been rendered by ὁ υἱὸσ τοῦ ἀνθρώπου, for each of these Greek phrases becomes *Barnāshā* in Aramaic.[1]

[1] To illustrate what I mean take the case of Mark viii 36, if we accept (as I think we ought) the reading τί γὰρ ὠφελήσει τὸν ἄνθρωπον. Here there is no linguistic reason why we should not understand the verse to have meant "What will it profit the Son of Man if he become Emperor of the whole world here, but lose His own personality?"

It is obvious that "the Man" can only have been used as a technical term in phrases where the context itself made the meaning fairly clear, for the evidence does not even attest "that Man" or any such explanatory word. A great deal has been written on this phrase ὁ υἱὸσ τοῦ ἀνθρώπου in recent years, and so difficult is it felt to be in many of the Gospel sayings, where it is found that some scholars are inclined to cut the knot by suggesting that later Christian scribes have introduced it in several places. "It became to them," i.e. these assumed Greek Christians, "merely the obscure and mysterious title which Jesus had traditionally used of Himself; and though it was not used in speaking of Him, was put into His own mouth on many inappropriate occasions." This is the suggestion of the Editors of *Beginnings* (i 383), and it is well to keep this possibility in mind. But the phrase itself is so strange and so little used by the second and third generation of Christians that I think we ought to reserve such explanations for passages where the phrase itself was suggested by the context. "The Sabbath was made for man, and not man for the Sabbath," said Jesus once. The Gospel of Mark goes on to make Him add: "So that the Son of Man is master of the Sabbath." I can very well believe that here the title "Son of Man" has been brought in by mistake, and that the word *Barnāshā* in the original Aramaic should have been rendered by ὁ ἄνθρωποσ and not ὁ υἱὸσ τοῦ ἀνθρώπου. The context shows that the intention of Jesus is to defend the action of the disciples who had plucked the ears of corn on a Sabbath, not to give them by His special authority a dispensation for an otherwise illegal act But here no doubt the word *Barnāshā* actually formed part of the Aramaic tradition. It is a much more hazardous theory to suppose that ὁ υἱὸσ τοῦ ἀνθρώπου was introduced into whole classes of sayings where the original had only a personal pronoun. I find it difficult to believe that Jesus never Himself connected His anticipations of suffering and rejection with the figure of "the Son of Man." In particular the passage Mark ix 9–13, so abrupt, so unliterary, so obscure in detail, however clear may be the general meaning, reads to me like reminiscences of a real conversation. I gather from it that Jesus did speak of "suffering" and of "the Son of Man" and that it was by the conjunction of the two things that Peter and his companions were puzzled.

It is worth while remembering that there are only two places in early Christian literature where Jesus is spoken of as "the Son of Man," outside the Gospels. One is the exclamation of Stephen who sees "the Son of Man" standing to receive him (Acts vii 56), and the other is in a saying of James, the "brother of the Lord," at the time of his martyrdom as reported by Hegesippus.[1] Both are exactly in the manner of the Gospels, and in the Hegesippus passage it is particularly difficult to imagine that the introduction of the phrase is due to a conscious imitation of the Gospel style. But even if these two passages be regarded

[1] Eusebius, *HE*, ii 23. The scribes and Pharisees ask James what "the Door of Jesus" is, and he answers: "What are you asking me about the Son of Man? He sits in heaven at the right hand of the Great Power, and is about to come on the clouds of heaven." See also below, p. 64.

as imitations, that implies something to imitate. What is really so difficult to believe is that the whole association of " suffering " with the Jewish apocalyptic figure of " the Man " (or " the Son of Man ") who was coming to judge the world is derived from a mere literary device.[1]

In another matter, concerning the idea of the Suffering Servant in Isaiah, I rejoice to find myself in essential agreement with the Editors of *Beginnings*, though indeed we are together in a minority. From what did Jesus derive the conviction that He was destined to suffer, to be rejected, to be killed ? The popular answer is that He

---

[1] It is conceivable that the wording of Acts vii 56 is due to " Luke," perhaps helped by reminiscence from historical knowledge of the circumstances of the death of James the Just. Certainly " Luke " has at least once introduced the actual mention of " the Son of Man " with noble literary effect, viz. in Luke xxi 36, a passage where it did not actually stand in his source (Mark xiii 35-37). But this is only a matter of phraseology and style, not of matter ; the idea was fully present in the source.

It should be added that in Rev. i 13, xiv 14, ὅμοιον υἱὸν ἀνθρώπου merely means " in human form," by an imitation of Biblical style. In xiv 14 the personage does not seem to be Christ.

identified Himself with the Suffering Servant of the LORD depicted by the Prophets, in other words that He derived it from a study of Isaiah liii. " The argument in favour of [this] theory is that it is consistent with Christian tradition, and that there seems no other literary source to account for the facts. The strongest argument against it is that there is no clear reference to the Suffering Servant in the early strata of the Gospels, though the writers were not prone to conceal their opinion when they saw a fulfilment of prophecy. It is of course immaterial for this question whether the amplification of the idea conveyed by the name Son of Man so as to include suffering was made by Jesus, foreseeing His own sufferings, or by His disciples afterwards. The point is that it was the knowledge of the Passion, whether prophetic or historic, not the interpretation of Isaiah liii, which produced the Gospel narrative " (*Beginnings*, i 383).

It seems to me that this is very well put. That Jesus was familiar with the words of the Prophets which were read in the synagogue every Sabbath day is of course self-evident.

The sign of Jonah, the Son of Man coming with the clouds, the people who honour with their lips though their heart is far from God, the worm that dies not and the fire unquenched,—these and many other striking phrases come straight out of the Prophets and other books of the canonical Scriptures. And if, as I believe, Matt. xxv 31–46 is to be taken as a genuine utterance of Jesus, then we must go on and allow for the influence of the Similitudes of Enoch upon the forms of His imagery. All the more remarkable is it, therefore, that the only clear use of Isaiah liii in any saying actually ascribed to Jesus is the quotation of ver. 12 in Luke xxii 37, a saying which in its context suggests that He hardly regarded the passage as specifically " Messianic."[1]

After the moving events of the Passion it did not take long for some Christians to see the correspondence with Isaiah liii. In the Gospel of Matthew (viii 17), in 1 Peter (ii 22–24), and less markedly in Hebrews (ix 28),

---

[1] It is sometimes asserted that Mark x 45 ($\tau\dot{\eta}\nu$ $\psi\upsilon\chi\dot{\eta}\nu$ $\alpha\dot{\upsilon}\tau o\hat{\upsilon}$ $\lambda\dot{\upsilon}\tau\rho o\nu$ $\dot{\alpha}\nu\tau\dot{\iota}$ $\pi o\lambda\lambda\hat{\omega}\nu$) shows the influence of the Hebrew text of Isa. liii 10*b*, 11*b*, but the expressions are very different.

verses from the chapter are quoted, expressly with the familiar Christian interpretation. In the next generation the whole chapter is quoted in full by Clement of Rome. But in no work is the Christian application made clearer than in the Lucan writings, particularly in the story of Philip and the Ethiopian eunuch (Acts viii 32f). On the other hand Paul and the Fourth Evangelist only quote it for ver. 1 ("LORD, who hath believed our report?"), a mere rhetorical use, not a Messianic application (Rom. x 16, John xii 38), and there seems little evidence that the writer of the N.T. Apocalypse paid any special attention to the chapter.[1]

The distribution of the two classes here is quite significant. On the one side are Luke, Hebrews, "1 Peter," the editor of the First Gospel; on the other are Paul, "John," and the Apocalyptist, together with the silence of Mark and of anything that could be grouped under "Q." That is to say, the writers who use the Greek Bible

[1] Rev. v 6, xiii 8, speak of a Lamb slain, but the imagery (e.g. the seven eyes) does not suggest the use of Isa. liii. In Rev. xiv 5 the use is non-Messianic ("*their* mouth").

exclusively are on one side, while those who, like St. Paul, have access to Semitic forms and interpretations of the Old Testament are on the other.

This is significant enough. It is enough to create a strong presumption that the application of Isaiah liii as a prediction of the Passion of Jesus was the work of Gentile Christians, familiar only with the Bible in Greek. But it does not stand alone. I venture to claim that the whole of what may for convenience be called the παῖσ θεοῦ Christology, the theory that sees in the passages about " the Servant of the Lord " in the latter half of Isaiah a prophecy of Jesus and His career is also the work of Greek-speaking believers, and therefore did not proceed from the earliest Christian circle, including the Apostles, which was of course an Aramaic-speaking community.

The matter is worth considering rather fully, because a neglect or misconception of the linguistic facts has caused certain passages in the Acts and other early Christian literature to be regarded as primitive Christian theology and Christology, whereas they really mark a stage which, though early, is not quite primitive.

Later Christian formulas speak of Jesus Christ as the Son of God (ὁ υἱὸσ τοῦ θεοῦ), not in the internal, psychological sense in which, as we have seen, the term is used in the story of the Temptation, but in a substantial, quasi-physical connotation. When therefore in the Acts, especially in what is given as the prayers of the earliest believers, and again in certain ancient Christian documents, mostly liturgical, such as the Didaché, we find in place of ὁ υἱὸσ τοῦ θεοῦ such phrases as "Thy holy child Jesus,"[1] it was natural to think we were in the presence of something really primitive. If, however, we look from the other end we shall arrive at a different conclusion.

The matter can be stated in a single sentence. The "servant of the LORD," "My servant," etc., is in Hebrew "the LORD's *slave*," "My *slave*." In the Greek translation of Isaiah, this notion, not very attractive to Greek ears, was not unsuitably softened by rendering '*ebed*, i.e. "slave," by παῖσ,

[1] E.g. Acts iv 30, τοῦ ἁγίου παιδόσ σου Ἰησοῦ.

a word which, like "boy" in English, means both *son* and *servant*. But this is peculiar to the Greek Bible. Now the earliest believers may very well have started with a "low" Christology, but I do not think that any of them, whether Greek or Jew, ever thought of Jesus, their Master, as God's slave. It is true that in certain passages it is clear that the Prophet is thinking of Israel, God's chosen Nation, but still the word that is used in the Hebrew means "slave," and that must have been enough to prevent Aramaic-speaking Christians like St. Peter or rabbinically schooled Christians like St. Paul from regarding the prophetic figure as a direct type of Jesus. With the Greek-speaking Christians it was different. There was nothing in the Greek Bible to show that the Servant (or Son) of the LORD spoken of by Isaiah was a bondservant, a slave, and so they applied the phrases used of the Servant to Jesus. This stage is represented in Acts: it is a very early stage of Greek-speaking Christianity, but it is not quite primitive or apostolic.

What did the earliest disciples call Jesus? How did they address Him? How did they speak of Him to others? The answer to the one of these questions is simple. The disciples were respectful and called Him "Sir." The corresponding Semitic word is *Rabbi*, but it is useful to begin with its English equivalent, because it may serve to remind us that not every respectful form of address can be used as an appellation. *Rabbi* means literally "My great one": there was another form, *Rabbūnī*,[1] of much the same meaning, which occurs in Mark x 51, John xx 16. The "scribes," i.e the learned expounders of the sacred Scriptures and Traditions, were already in the time of Jesus the religious guides of the Jews; after the Destruction of Jerusalem and the collapse of the Jewish State they became their only religious guides. Consequently the Jewish leader of religion and the teacher of religious lore became synonymous. The men to whom Jews said "Sir" became professed

---

[1] The (later) Hebrew form is *Ribbōnī*. The Christian Syriac form of this word is *Rabbūlī*, just as in Syriac "Reuben" becomes *Rubīl*.

CHRISTIAN BEGINNINGS 43

Teachers, and Teachers only, and the word *Rabbi* acquired something of the connotation of a schoolmaster. No doubt Jesus was a religious Teacher: Mark vii 9ff, and especially 18ff, shows Him in the character of a Jewish "Rabbi," teaching a very interesting and peculiar *Halācha*.[1] But He was not only a Teacher to Peter and Peter's companions. The earliest rendering indeed of *Rabbi* as a form of address to Him is Διδάσκαλε, which does mean "Teacher," but I venture to think that neither this nor "Rabbi" gives so good an equivalent as "Sir," for owing to its later use "Rabbi" carries with it a suggestion of technical learning, not to say pedantry, that is quite foreign to the Gospel contexts. St. Luke felt this, and kept Διδάσκαλε for the speeches of the opponents of Jesus (who really were asking Him questions as a Rabbi), substituting Ἐπιστάτα when disciples were speaking, because, as Bretschneider said long ago, they called Jesus "Rabbi" not from the fact that

---

[1] I refer particularly to the rule that ritual pollution comes not from food, but from issues and excrement. I believe this was intended as a *rule*, and the moral application was a *deduction*.

He was a teacher, but because of His authority. When the Evangelist Matthew is retelling the story of the entry of Jesus into Jerusalem he makes the crowds say " This is the Prophet Jesus from Nazareth of Galilee " : he does not make them say " This is Rabbi Jesus."[1]

In John xiii 13 Jesus says to the Apostles " Ye call me *Master* and *Lord* " : here *Master* is ὁ διδάσκαλοσ and *Lord* is ὁ κύριοσ. In 1 Cor. xii 3, on the other hand, St. Paul gives the formula Κύριοσ Ἰησοῦσ, " Jesus is *Kyrios*," as if it almost required special inspiration to utter it; and in Rom. x 9 the same formula is given as containing in itself the essentials of Christian theology. It is obvious that κύριοσ, " Lord," is here being used in two senses, and it has appeared from the investigations of the last twenty years that a full discussion of it would lead us very far in the field of Comparative Religion and the Mystery-cults of the later Roman

---

[1] It is perhaps worth remarking that *Ya Rabbi!* a very common Arabic exclamation, means *O my Lord God!* It is only in post-Biblical Hebrew and Jewish Aramaic that *Rabbi* has any scholastic flavour, and it is not very clear whether it had acquired this scholastic flavour before New Testament times.

Empire. I need only here indicate the chief points of interest.

In John xiii 13 what is meant, no doubt, is " Ye call me *Rabbi* and *Mārī*." As we have seen, *Rabbi* and *Rabbuni* (*Ribbōnī*) were Jewish titles of respect : Jael said *Ribḅōnī* to Sisera, according to the Aramaic Targum (Judges iv 18). But the servants of Naaman, according to the Targum (2 Kings v 13), said to him *Mārī*, i.e. " My Master," "*Domine mi.*" This was quite correct ; no doubt they really were Naaman's slaves and Naaman was their master. But it seems to have been used as a respectful form of address by others than slaves: according to Philo (*in Flacc.* 6) Μάρι(ν) was said to a Prince.[1] There is therefore not much reason to doubt that some persons may have addressed Jesus as *Mari*. Mark makes the Syrophenician Gentile woman say to Him κύριε, and it is the only time this form of address is used in that Gospel. In Matthew and Luke κύριε is much commoner, but it is remarkable that where it occurs in the para-

[1] So also in Matt. xxvii 63 the chief priests say κύριε to Pilate. Another instance is Dan. iv 16.

bles of Jesus it is usually where slaves are addressing their masters.[1] Martha says κύριε to Jesus, so does Zacchaeus, so does Peter, when he is prepared to follow Jesus to prison and when he is expecting an order to draw his sword. I cannot help feeling that in the Synoptic Gospels κύριε implies " Milord," rather than " Sir." The Fourth Gospel is different: here κύριε is " Sir," and no more, as is clear from John xii 21, xx 15.

But though enthusiastic admirers might from time to time say " Lord, Lord," to Jesus it is clear from Mark xiv 14 that before the Crucifixion, even at the latest period, the regular followers of Jesus spoke of Him to others as their Rabbi[2]—not exactly their " Teacher," but rather their " Chief." The Resurrection doubtless changed the terminology at once. The disciples who believed—and they were the nucleus of the future Church—were not at once provided

---

[1] Matt. xxi 30 is an exception : here a son replies to his father, but he is meant to speak in a subservient style.

[2] No doubt ὁ διδάσκαλοσ in Mark xiv 14 represents *Rabban*, i.e. " our Rabbi," as the Syriac has it.

with what we call a Christology, with an appropriate nomenclature for their mysterious Master. But they could have had no doubt that they were His men and women, they were His servants and He was their Lord.

The thing is almost self-evident, and it is no surprise to find our documents speaking of Jesus as κύριοσ in all stories of the post-Resurrection period, such as "God hath made Him both Lord and Christ, this Jesus" (Acts ii 36), and even "the Lord is risen indeed" (Luke xxiv 34). The remarkable fact is that so little use is otherwise made of κύριοσ as a title for our Lord in the Synoptic Gospels and that even the vocative κύριε is so discreetly employed. This is no new discovery: the evidence is indeed so familiar that its significance is liable to be forgotten or passed over. It certainly seems to me to be one of the many evidences that our traditions of the public career of Jesus are based ultimately on reminiscence and not upon creative religious fancy. And here, as elsewhere, the good historical tradition is mainly due to the influence of the Gospel of Mark: it was not indeed itself much read, but it moulded the language of the more popular Gospels according to Matthew and Luke.

The Fourth Gospel, here as elsewhere, goes its own peculiar way. St. Jude was content to describe himself as the slave of Christ though the brother of James (Jude 1), but the Fourth Evangelist will have none of this. Those who receive the True Light (he says) become not slaves of God but sons (John i 12), those who know the Truth are freemen (viii 32), it is only the sinner who is a slave (viii 34), so that Jesus will not call the disciples "slaves" but "friends" (xv 15). The correlative of slave (δοῦλοσ) is master or lord (κύριοσ); therefore the Evangelist is at pains not to lay stress on κύριοσ as a title for Jesus. He does allude to Him as "the Lord" (ὁ κύριοσ, xi 2), and doubtless this way of speaking of Jesus was current when he wrote. But the Pauline formula Κύριοσ 'Ιησοῦσ is not enough for him. When Thomas says "My Lord and my God" (ὁ κύριόσ μου καὶ ὁ θεόσ μου), what is implied really is "It *is* Jesus Himself, and now I recognize Him as Divine."

CHRISTIAN BEGINNINGS 49

In what I have been saying I have had in mind some of the results of the modern study of the "Mystery-religions" which flourished in the Greco-Roman world during the first three centuries of our era, the worship of Isis, of Attis, of Mithra. That these presented in religious theory and ritual practice some striking resemblance to Christianity was noticed by Christian Apologists in the 2nd century, and Justin Martyr explains the similarity by ascribing it to the ingenuity of evil demons.[1] One strong point of resemblance is this: Mithra was "Lord" to the worshipper of Mithra, Jesus was "Lord" to the Christian. This has been set forth at full length in a really great book, Bousset's *Kyrios Christos*,[2] but it seems to me that he has rather put the cart before the horse. The devotee of the special heathen cults called his Cult-hero "Lord" or κύριοσ, because he did regard himself as the slave of the Cult-hero: he belonged to his household. So also with the Christian. It is evident that this was not the state of things during the public career of Jesus, in

[1] Justin, *Ap.* I 66.   [2] See especially p. 119.

the time before the Crucifixion. The disciples were disciples, followers, adherents: some of them were really loyal and devoted, nevertheless they belonged to a movement rather than a sect.

But the case was different immediately afterwards. Whatever our views may be about the Resurrection there can be little doubt that St. Peter believed in it. Peter, and the little band that rallied round Peter, became convinced—and that almost at once—that Jesus was alive again, that some of them had seen Him alive, and that therefore it was worth while going on hoping and believing that He would return again in glory. The whole of Christian tradition asserts this much. Indeed it asserts very much more, but I have been careful to phrase my sentence to include what everyone would admit. Now this means that the believers were standing on a different plane to the mere disciples with regard to Jesus. As I said just now, they were not provided with a ready-made Christology, a set of terms or titles that exactly expressed their beliefs, beliefs which themselves were not yet fixed or developed. My point, an extremely simple and elementary one, is only this: that the very circumstances of men who continued to believe that God had still a great future in store for Jesus the Nazarene who had been crucified—pardon the crudity of my phrases—were different from followers of a masterful religious teacher from whom they hoped great things. It is not wonderful that these believers really did regard Him as their " Lord " rather than their Teacher, or even their Chief, and themselves as His Liegemen or subjects rather than as His companions.

This sounds to me reasonable and natural, indeed almost obvious; it is also what our documents tell us. But it is not the theory of Bousset, which I suppose is now dominant in critical circles. Bousset denies that the earliest believers at Jerusalem used the title " Lord " for Jesus. This is based on two considerations: (1) that ὁ κύριοσ, and even κύριε, are avoided in the more primitive sections of the Gospels, and (2) that *Mari* was not a regular form of Jewish address. It was therefore (according to this theory) reserved for the predominantly Greek-speaking and Gentile community of Antioch to adopt the new name *Kyrios* from the language of contemporary popular heathen religion. I venture to think the old-fashioned tradition is in this case more probable than the new theory. What remains, however, is the surprising avoidance of the title *Kyrios* in the Synoptic Gospels, with the partial exception of Luke. That Mark so entirely, and Matthew and Luke to so great an extent, have marked the difference between the conditions in the periods before and after the belief in the resurrection of Jesus as regards this matter of nomenclature is to me a singular indication of historical feeling on the part of our Evangelists, a feeling which is not at all shared by what we know of the writers of the apocryphal evangelical literature.

LECTURE II

ANY study of Christian beginnings must be largely occupied with the Book of Acts of Apostles, which forms the second volume to the Gospel of Luke. The first four volumes of the work of Professors Jackson and Lake, to which I have so often referred, are indeed directly concerned with the Book of Acts, the first two volumes being Prolegomena while the third is to give the Text and the fourth a Commentary. How much we owe to Acts is of course clear at once, when we try to continue the history of the Church after the narrative in Acts breaks off. When it breaks off we are at once plunged in darkness. What happened to St. Paul in Rome? What happened to St. Peter? How was the Church organized in Rome, in Antioch, in Alexandria, during the thirty years after their deaths? These are very simple and obvious questions, but we can give no certain answer to them, because our guide has failed us, and no other of the same sort has taken its place.

But if our subject be the Beginnings of Christianity a more serious difficulty still confronts us. The historical value of the Book of Acts itself has been seriously challenged, especially as an account of the earliest period, of the first organization of the believers in Jerusalem. That "Acts" contains at least some trustworthy historical information in the latter part is generally acknowledged. The journey of Paul to Jerusalem, his arrest by the Roman authority, his subsequent voyage to Rome as a prisoner, all this is accepted even by those who would say that the speeches at the trial were largely written up by the writer of Acts. What is not so universally accepted by responsible critics is the picture of the early days of the Church in Jerusalem.

Let me say at once that a good part of the hesitation and diffidence of the critics is more or less justified. We cannot suppose that "Acts" is more accurate than "Luke," and if in studying the Gospel history we again and again follow Mark rather than Luke as a guide to our own reconstruction of the course of events, or perceive only too clearly that Luke has blurred the sharp outlines of the document upon which his own narrative is based, we cannot hope that he will always be a safe guide in " Acts " where we have no Mark to check his statements.

What is wanted above all in studying the Book of Acts is some criterion, some external authority to corroborate or to question the main outlines of the picture there drawn. The matter chiefly concerns the Christianity of Jerusalem and of the believers, if such there were, in the rest of the land of Israel. It has seemed to me therefore that we can best begin our study by bringing together the historical notices of this Jewish, Semitic Christianity. It is not much that survives, but it will at least serve to put our ideas straight.

First of all come the few but valuable data to be picked up from the letters of St. Paul. In Gal. i 16-19 Paul tells us that about the time of his own conversion Peter was to be found in Jerusalem, and James, " the Lord's brother," was already a convert and a person of consideration among the believers. Further, Jerusalem is the only named centre of this Jewish Christianity; " churches of God in Judea " are referred to but never named;[1] and not even in 2 Cor. xi 32, where Paul is speaking of his adventures in Damascus, is a Christian community mentioned as established or organized there. Whatever the date of Rom. xv may be, the impression we get is that the community in or about Jerusalem was the only one of any importance in St. Paul's eyes.

From Gal. ii we learn that " James " and " Cephas " and " John " were the chief men of the Jerusalem believers when Paul went up to Jerusalem with Titus. *James* is no doubt James the Lord's brother, and the position in which St. Paul puts him, together with the notice in Gal. ii 12, makes it clear that he was already the recognized head of the society. *Cephas* is, of course, Peter. *John* may be the son of Zebedee: it is also conceivable that he is the mysterious John the Elder who afterwards lived at Ephesus. The date of the Galatian letter is disputed:

[1] Gal. i 22, 1 Thess. ii 14.

CHRISTIAN BEGINNINGS

I believe that it is really early, and that this visit of Paul with Titus corresponds to Acts xi 30, rather than to Acts xv and the so-called Apostolic Council. In other words, on the great and burning question of circumcision the Jerusalem community had not yet come to a final decision, but the account of Paul shows the leaders as friendly to him. It shows Peter as more than half a liberal and James as at least inclined to give way to the new view. It was not the leaders who were fanatical and irreconcilable.[1]

What sort of a man, then, was this James, "the brother of the Lord"? For answer we may go with some confidence to the famous story of his martyrdom, quoted by Eusebius (*HE*, ii 23) from Hegesippus. It will be convenient to quote it here rather fully, as several points in it seem to me to deserve special notice. Hegesippus says:

"Now there succeeded to the charge of the Church (in Jerusalem), with the Apostles,

[1] "It is one of the mistakes of the Tübingen School that it did not recognize that Peter, not only in Acts but also in the Pauline Epistles, is on the Hellenistic, not the Hebrew side" (*Beginnings*, vol. i 312). This admirable sentence may be taken to mark the end of a long controversy.

the Lord's brother James, known as 'James the Righteous' by everybody from the times of the Lord to our own, to distinguish him from the many called James. Now this man was holy from his mother's womb: no wine or strong drink did he drink nor did he eat anything that had life, no razor touched his head, he used no oil and never had a bath. To this man alone was it lawful to enter the sanctuary (τὰ ἅγια). Moreover he never wore wool, but only linen garments. And alone he used to go into the Temple (τὸν ναόν), and be found on his knees beseeching forgiveness for the people, till his knees grew like a camel's through being always kneeling in prayer to God and begging forgiveness for the people. And indeed owing to his excessive righteousness † James was called Righteous and The people's Defence,†[1] as the Prophets make clear about him.

"Certain then of the seven Sects among

---

[1] This seems to me to be the general meaning of the clause: ἐκαλεῖτο δίκαιοσ καιωβλιασ· ὅ ἐστιν Ἑλληνιστὶ περιοχὴ, κ.τ.λ. was very likely what Eusebius wrote, but I doubt if it was what Hegesippus intended. *Oblias* means nothing at all: on the other hand it looks very like a corruption of Ἰακώβ, *plus* something else now hopelessly corrupted.

the people, about whom I [i.e. Hegesippus] have written above, were asking him, 'What is the Door of Jesus?' And he was saying that He was the Saviour. From which some believed that Jesus is the Christ, but the above-mentioned Sects neither believed in a resurrection nor in One coming to render to each one according to his deeds: such as did believe did so owing to James. As therefore many even of the ruling classes were believing there was an uproar of the Jews and scribes and Pharisees, saying that all the people were in danger of expecting Jesus as the Christ ('Ιησοῦν τὸν Χριστὸν προσδοκᾶν)."

Accordingly James is asked to give his testimony at the Passover to allay this unreasonable superstition. They set him on the "pinnacle of the Temple" and say (so Hegesippus continues): "'Righteous one, whom we ought all to obey, since the people are going astray after Jesus who was crucified, tell us what is the Door of Jesus?' And he answered with a loud voice, 'Why do you ask me about the Son of Man?[1]

[1] *Sic.*, περὶ τοῦ υἱοῦ τοῦ ἀνθρώπου (without 'Ιηοῦ). So the best MS. and the Syriac and the Latin.

He sits in heaven at the right hand of the Great Power and He is to come on the clouds of heaven!'" Many were edified, says Hegesippus, and gave glory to God at the witness of James and were saying, " Hosanna to the Son of David," but the scribes and Pharisees were much displeased, and they plotted his death, "fulfilling the scripture written in Isaiah, ' Let us take away the Righteous one because he is no use for us; wherefore the fruit of their works they shall eat.' " [1] Whereupon they stoned him, and though James prays, like Stephen, for his murderers he is finally killed by a blow from a fuller's club. " And they buried him on the spot by the Temple, and his memorial stone remains by the Temple."

This is the tale told by Hegesippus. Obviously it is not the report of an eyewitness, but the form in which the death of the great hero of the Christians at Jerusalem was related at Jerusalem in the first half of the 2nd century. Moreover the tale as given by Hegesippus quotes the Greek

[1] Isa. iii 10, according to the LXX, but with ἄρωμεν instead of δήσωμεν.

version of Isaiah iii 10, a passage where that version differs widely from the Hebrew. Either therefore the whole form of the story is due to Hegesippus himself, writing not before A.D. 160, or (as is more probable) he is quoting the tale from the Greek-speaking and Gentile Christian community of Aelia Capitolina, a community discontinuous both in race and language from that over which James himself presided.

Nevertheless I think we can learn a good deal from this famous story. We can learn what kind of impression James made, what manner of man he was. The portrait is easy enough to recognize. He is the normal, almost conventional, Holy Man of the East, as normal and conventional to that type as Jesus was unconventional. James's manner of life is ascetic and altogether dominated by the expected advent of the Messiah. Not only is he a life-long Nazirite: he spends his days in the precincts of the Temple, supplicating for the sins of Israel. Hegesippus does not specify the crucifixion of Jesus, nor need we: it is the sin of the people in general, the sin that delays the glorious coming of the Kingdom of God and keeps Israel under the domination of the Gentiles.

No doubt James regarded the Law as permanent, at least until the Kingdom of God should come. But, we may ask, did James himself keep the Law? Did he offer sacrifices and eat the Passover, year after year, as the Feast came round? Did he pay the sacred tithe?

I venture to suggest that the abstinence of St. James was not exclusively directed to the mortification of the flesh. He may indeed have been a Nazirite from the beginning, like Samson of old, as Hegesippus implies, but he does not say that he was a vegetarian from the beginning. Now we know very little of the details of Jewish Christian religion. No doubt, as I said before, in a rather different but not quite dissimilar context, they did not have a developed Christology, but I do not suppose that the idea of "Christ our Passover" was exclusively Pauline. Certainly the Ebionites make Jesus say in their Gospel, " I came to destroy the sacrifices " : [1] this may be

[1] Epiph., *Haer.* 30.

CHRISTIAN BEGINNINGS

taken as unexceptionable evidence that some at least of the Jewish Christian schools of thought had a difficulty in combining the old sacrificial worship with their new belief that Jesus was the chosen of God.

But there was one way of escape for the non-Pauline believer. He might believe that the Law continued to be binding till the Return of the Messiah, but what of that? The Interim would surely be short, and meanwhile he could abstain from the chief matters with which Ritual was concerned. He who abstained from meat altogether would not be called upon to eat the Paschal Lamb; he who had no land or possessions was not concerned with the Laws of Tithe. St. James seems to me to have been such a one. Like Jesus, the Temple was to him the House of Prayer: he was Righteous, he kept the Law, so far as it applied to him, but Sacrifices were a matter for the flesh-eaters and Tithe for the rich.

With this view of St. James goes very well the story quoted by Jerome from the Gospel according to the Hebrews, that James " had vowed he would not eat bread from the hour that he had drunk the cup of the Lord, till he saw Him rising from the dead," and that the Lord appeared to him and said " My Brother, eat thy bread, for the Son of Man hath risen from them that sleep " (*De Viris Illustr.* s.v. " Jacobus "). It is the same James—the man of vows about eating and drinking, into whose legend the term " Son of Man " slips in so easily.

A remark or two about the Christology of James, as revealed in the Hegesippus story, may not be out of place. The words put into the mouth of this first Bishop of Jerusalem are surely very odd. The tale is the witness of James to Jesus, for which he is gloriously martyred. The effect of his witness is that many come to believe that Jesus is the Christ; but James carefully avoids saying so. Indeed the whole story seems pointless, unless the hitherto known utterances of James had been such as to make it reasonable for the adversaries to hope that when directly interrogated he would not assert Jesus to be the Christ. James had taught that Jesus was the Saviour, that through His Door believers might attain safety.[1] But when asked formally about Jesus, he answers only about "the Son of Man," in a phrase that might have been penned by the author of the Similitudes of Enoch.

I have made a point of this, because it also deserves to be taken into consideration when we are considering the very curious question of the authorship of the Epistle of James. The problems presented by this work are in many ways unlike that of the other canonical and deutero-canonical writings, and deserve a few moments' special consideration. The ordinary English reader of the Epistle of James is troubled by few doubts as to its authenticity. There is an air of rugged freedom about it, of interest in practical ethics and the poorer classes, that recalls the Synoptic Gospels rather than the other New Testament Epistles. Theological dogma and sacerdotalism are conspicuous by their absence. If the document be a forgery, we feel, why was it ever accepted? What stage of second-

[1] Cf. Luke xiii 24ff.

century thinking can it be supposed to represent? Why should it have been written? and why should it have been accepted as canonical?

When we go on to read the Epistle in Greek the impression is not so favourable. It is written in better, more literary Greek than we should have expected from the unshaven devotee who haunted the Temple colonnades. The vocabulary used is considerable and strikes one as of a slightly more classical grade than that of the rest of the New Testament: the writer had been to school, or at least had read some Greek books. Moreover he used the Greek Bible: Jas. v 4, with its allusion to the ears of the Lord Sabaoth, clearly goes back to the LXX text of Isaiah v 9. Is this what we should have expected from James the Just?

Further, the Epistle cannot be said to be endorsed as genuine by the consensus of Christian antiquity. It was not in the genuine Old Latin; there is no trace of it in the West till the 4th century. Nor was it in the Old Syriac, for there is no trace of it in Syriac literature before the time of Rabbula

(411–435).[1] The earliest certain reference to it is by Origen, *in Joan. xix* 23, a passage written after his arrival in Palestine. This Commentary on St. John is the first Christian work in which reference is made to " the Places," the sacred sites and the visits of Christians to them, afterwards such an important feature in Palestinian Church life. The inference to be drawn is that the Epistle of James was preserved by Palestinian Christians, i.e. most probably by the Gentile, Greek-speaking Church of Aelia.

It should be added that James's chair was religiously preserved by the bishops of Aelia-Jerusalem (Euseb. *HE* vii 19). All these indications seem to me to fit very well together. The Church of Aelia had really the worst pedigree of any. " The break in continuity between Jerusalem and Aelia must have been absolute. . . . The Christians of Aelia, if at first there were any of them at all, would have been not only Gentiles by race, but inimical, by the very

---

[1] No lesson is taken from St. James in the earliest extant Syriac Lectionary, which goes back to Rabbula's time (Burkitt, *The Early Syriac Lectionary System*, p. 22).

fact of their consenting to settle in the pagan city, to all that pertained to Judaism or even to Jewish Christianity." So writes C. H. Turner in his admirable discussion of the early episcopal list of Jerusalem.[1] He goes on to say: " Few chapters in the history of the early Church are more curious than the rise of the rulers of this once insignificant body to the fifth place in the precedence of the catholic hierarchy as ratified by the Council of Chalcedon: and though it was a far cry to the recognition of the Patriarchate, yet the movement by which the Church of Aelia began to see in itself the inheritor of the august traditions of the Holy City must have had its roots back in the second century."[2] In other words, the Gentile Church in the new pagan Jerusalem was rather like a new purchaser that has bought the Old Manor House, who after a while begins to collect old family portraits and souvenirs—coming at last to believe himself the genuine heir of the old line. Let us not be too hard on them. The chair of St. James, so far as we know, has disappeared,

[1] *Journal of Theol. Studies* i 550.   [2] *Ibid.* i 551.

but the Letter remains, and the circumstances of its preservation seem to me to give a clue to the internal evidences both of authenticity and of spuriousness that it presents.

The original was no doubt in Aramaic; what we have is a rendering, not very literal, into Greek.[1] The classical, non-Biblical expressions, such as "the wheel of genesis" (iii 6) reflect the culture of the translator, not the speech of St. James, and the Septuagintal language of the Scripture allusions are the translator's work also. The original was evidently an exhortation to a particular congregation, well known to James (ii 2ff, iv 1, v 4); the translator has turned it into a general Epistle to the Twelve Tribes in the Dispersion—thereby incidentally including his fellow-churchmen in Gentile Aelia Capitolina. Is it not significant that in Hegesippus's account of the martyrdom of James he speaks of "all the *tribes*" coming up to the feast of the

---

[1] In James iii 6 is it not possible that ὁ κόσμοσ is a translator's error, עלמא for מעלנא "entrance"? That is, the tongue among our members is that whereby wickedness, ἀδικία, *enters* (see further, ver. 10).

Passover? Indeed, for aught we know, Hegesippus himself may have been the translator; but even if that be too simple a solution to be true, I think it not unreasonable to regard the translator as having been one of the same community, and of the same tendencies.

The main result of this long excursus is to suggest that in the "Epistle of James" we have a free Greek rendering of an original Aramaic discourse made by James, the brother of the Lord, to some Jewish-Christian community, very likely that of Jerusalem itself. It was rescued from oblivion by the Greek-speaking Gentile-Christian Church of Aelia, when they were beginning to adopt St. James as their ecclesiastical ancestor. To the same community is due the form in which the story of the martyrdom of James has come down to us, from which story we may gather that James lived the life of a Temple devotee, dominated by the thought of the approaching End of all things: his manner of life, that of the Oriental ascetic, gave him even in his lifetime a great réputation as a saint. He was undoubtedly both a Jew and a

Christian, but he seems to have maintained a certain independence of view. As a Christian he believed in the Divine mission of Jesus, and taught that through Him men were saved from the wrath to come, but he seems to have been unwilling to apply to Jesus the title of Messiah,[1] though he was killed for his loyalty to Him. As a Jew he kept strictly to the Law, but his ascetic manner of life removed him from most of the situations in which the ordinary Jewish Christian must have been in a difficulty.

The ordinary Jewish Christians—where did they live, and what were their opinions? I am afraid the answer must be that we know very little about them. Of one thing indeed we may be sure, that the Destruction of Jerusalem and the Jewish State by Titus in A.D. 70 was even more disastrous for their religion than for the ordinary Jews. The Jew who despaired after the Jewish State had perished was confronted with the alternative

[1] See Hegesippus's account above, and the silence of the Epistle, except for i 1 and the broken construction of ii 1. Possibly the word *Meshiḥa* had to James the connotation of a worldly king, as suggested in Luke xxiii 2.

of giving up his religion altogether: the Jewish Christian had also the easier alternative of becoming an ordinary Christian. I cannot doubt that a good many Jewish Christian survivors of the Jewish War abandoned the specifically Jewish part of their religion altogether. Jewish Christianity after A.D. 70 seems to have been an unimportant survival, which persisted only in a few districts of Palestine and the immediate neighbourhood.

We hear from Talmudic sources a little about the *Minim*, or heretics, who are usually considered to be Jewish Christians. A short chronological account of what is known of these *Minim*—unfortunately it comes to very little—is given by G. F. Moore in *Beginnings*, i 319f. We learn more from a neglected passage out of St. Jerome's commentary on Isaiah. In his exposition of Isaiah viii 14 (*in petram scandali duabus domibus Israel*) he tells us that the Christian Nazaraeans interpret this phrase of the two schools of Shammai and Hillel, and they mention as their successors, Meir and Johanan ben Zakkai, Akiba and Aquila,

CHRISTIAN BEGINNINGS

Eliezer ben Hyrkanus, Tarphon (written Telphon), and Jose the Galilean. Further, by a spiteful perversion they interpreted Shammai to mean " devastator " and Hillel " profane " (i.e. Ḥillel for Hillel), and said that by their Mishna (δευτερώσεισ) they had devastated and profaned the Law.[1]

The importance of this passage consists in the light which it throws upon the culture of these Nazaraeans, i.e. the Jewish Christians of Aleppo who survived to St. Jerome's day and allowed him to copy out their " Gospel according to the Hebrews." I do not think that there is another passage in any of the Church Fathers which betrays so much acquaintance with Talmudic Judaism. It is true that Johanan b. Zakkai is placed too

[1] Hieron. *in Isai.* viii 14 (123): Duas domus Nazaraei, qui ita Christum recipiunt ut observationis Legis ueteris non amittant, duas familias interpretantur *Sammai* et *Hellel*, ex quibus orti sunt scribae et Pharisaei, quorum suscepit scholam *Acibas* quem magistrum *Aquilae* proselyti autumant, et post eum *Mehir*, cui successit *Iohannan filius Zachaei*, et post eum *Eliezer*, et per ordinem *Telphon* et rursum *Ioseph Galilaeus*, et usque ad captivitatem Ierusalem *Iosue*. Sammai igitur et Hellel non multo priusquam Dominus nasceretur orti sunt Iudaea, quorum prior *dissipator* interpretatur, sequens *profanus*: eo quod per traditiones et δευτερώσεισ suas Legis praescripta dissipauerit atque maculauerit.

late, but that may be due to Jerome's faulty transmission of a string of unfamiliar names. These last survivals of Jewish Christianity may thus be regarded as a kind of Jewish Dissenters. Their culture is Jewish, they are consciously in opposition to the leaders of the established Jewish religion. Another passage (Hieron. *in Isai.* ix 1) shows that they were proud of the missionary labours of St. Paul, but the great Catholic Church of the Empire seems to have been simply alien to their circle of interests.

Such no doubt were the *Minim*, of whom we read in Talmudic literature. It is a pity that this literature tells us so little positive about them. There is, however, one point that is clear, and I bring it forward here because it is not noticed in *Beginnings*, i 320, the passage to which I referred just now. The point is, that the sacred book of the *Minim* was called *Evangelion*. This appears from the amusing story of R. Eliezer and Salome sister of Gamaliel the younger (about A.D. 100),[1] and also from a saying of R. Meir

[1] Talmud, b. Shabb. 116 *a b*: given in full by Neubauer, *Studia Biblica* i 58.

referred to by G. F. Moore. In both these passages the "Gospel" is spoken of as עון גליון *'awon gillaion*, i.e. "writing-tablet's sin," an intentional perversion of *Evangelion*. But this is a Greek word. It is unlikely that an original collection of the words or deeds of Jesus made by the Aramaic-speaking believers in Palestine would have been called εὐαγγέλιον, so that even the Talmudic references to Palestinian Christians at the end of the first century A.D. testify to the comparative originality of the *Greek* Gospels. With this piece of evidence may be associated the fact that the "Gospel according to the Hebrews," as received by the Nazaraeans and quoted by Jerome, appears to be a particular form of our Gospel according to Matthew, itself an adaptation of the far more primitive Gospel according to Mark.

The main result of all that I have been saying is, I fear, somewhat negative, but it will have done enough if it has shown how strong the evidence is for connecting Jewish

Christianity before the Destruction of Jerusalem with Jerusalem itself, and how little evidence there is for any Christianity in Palestine elsewhere than in Jerusalem. This is a fact of the greatest importance when we go on to examine the account of the earliest days of the Church as given in Acts.

On p. 171 of the second volume of *The Beginnings of Christianity* it is remarked by the Editors that " a more subtle theory [than that of Johannes Weiss about the Resurrection-appearances] has been suggested, though never fully expounded, by F. C. Burkitt." It will therefore not be out of place to explain my view at some length.

It is not the question of the reality or subjectivity of the appearances of Jesus to His disciples after the Crucifixion. On that great subject I have only one remark to make, namely, that the subsequent effect of these alleged appearances is exactly what one would expect if something really out of the common had occurred. Let me explain what I mean by a contrary instance. The Feeding of the Multitudes is a well-attested event, as the attestation of such a thing goes.

It is possible to get rid of the feeding of the four thousand by asserting that it is only a "doubtlet" of the feeding of the five thousand; but if so, you only add a fresh independent witness to the feeding of the five thousand. Moreover the story is not an isolated event, like the Gerasene demoniac: it is intertwined with the whole narrative, with the retirement of Jesus after John the Baptist's execution, with the subsequent retirement *via* Gennesaret to "the borders of Tyre," and also with the theories of some early Christians about sanctions for their Sacred Meals. You cannot just cut the story out of the Gospel because it seems incredible, seeing that it is embedded into the fabric of the narrative. Yet the same document that tells us of these wonderful feedings tells us also that soon afterwards, when provisions ran short during a not very extensive or out-of-the-way voyage, the same disciples who had witnessed the feedings were alarmed for their dinner (Mark viii 13-21). The conclusion is obvious: the wonderful meals had not impressed those who witnessed them, as they would have if they had been as wonderful as the narrative implies. So we are justified in " rationalizing " the narratives, in seeking a more or less rationalistic account of them, in explaining the miraculous details away.

But if this line of argument be sound for the feeding of the five thousand, exactly the opposite is the case with the Resurrection. The traditional accounts of the Resurrection-appearances to the various disciples are confused and inconsistent; it is not very easy to construct any consistent narrative about them and impossible to gather all the tales into a consistent narrative. But the general result upon those who are said to have seen the Lord is what we might have expected from a " miraculous " experience: they are convinced by what they see, and remain convinced. The same, it may be remarked, is true of the " vision " of St. Paul; it leaves an abiding effect on his will and outlook.

It seems to me therefore that the historian is justified in postulating something surprising, some event following the Crucifixion of Jesus which is not quite explicable. Whether Peter and Paul were mistaken in their belief that they had seen the Lord

Jesus is at this time of day, strictly speaking, unprovable ; what I do think we are bound to recognize is that they were fully convinced that they had seen Him.

But the question with which we are now chiefly concerned is the place of these appearances. *Where* was Peter convinced that he had seen his Lord alive ? The special interest of this question is not so much theological or philosophical as historical. It concerns the character and credibility of the Book of Acts as an historical document, and is of the first importance for anyone who wishes to construct for himself a picture of the first beginnings of the Christian community.

The documents upon which we have to go are only five : St. Paul (1 Cor. xv 3-8), Matthew, Mark, Luke with Acts, and John. Thirty years of scrutiny has not established the claim of the " Gospel of Peter " to be an independent witness, or even to preserve any fresh element of historical value. And, as I have already indicated, I do not consider the " Nazaraean " Gospel, called also the Gospel according to the Hebrews, to be a really independent witness. It does give details of an appearance of the risen Christ to James the Just, but no detail of place is preserved, so that even if this story be based after all on independent tradition it gives us no information about the subject of our inquiry.

The same must be said of the most ancient of our five authorities, for St. Paul does not tell us where the Lord was seen, whether in Jerusalem or in Galilee.

Of the Four Gospels the two extreme views are presented in the Gospel according to Matthew and in the Lucan writings. According to Luke the disciples never got far from Jerusalem after the Crucifixion and the Lord was seen by them in or near Jerusalem. According to Matthew "the eleven disciples went into Galilee, unto the mountain where Jesus had appointed them" (xxviii 16), and there the Lord charged them to teach all nations and baptize them in the Name of the Trinity.

The Gospel of Mark breaks off at xvi 8 in the middle of a paragraph, just after the Women have failed to find the body of Jesus and have been told by the "youth" at the tomb that Jesus was leading them, or going before them, into Galilee (Προάγει ὑμᾶσ εἰσ τὴν Γαλιλαίαν). This is an echo of Mark xiv 28, where Jesus tells the Twelve, after quoting Zech. xiii 7 to warn them that they will all be scattered, that nevertheless when He is raised up He will be in Galilee before them, or will lead them into Galilee (προάξω ὑμᾶσ εἰσ τὴν Γ.). What Mark went on to tell in the part of his work that is lost we cannot strictly say, but at least these two texts could hardly have been inserted by the Evangelist without leading up either to an appearance in Galilee, or to some explanation why it did not take place.

The Fourth Gospel here as elsewhere is peculiar. In John xx 19–23 Jesus appears to the disciples on the evening of Easter Sunday, obviously in Jerusalem. In John xx 26ff He appears again on the Sunday following. The way in which the story is told leaves the impression that the Apostles are still in Jerusalem: otherwise why should the doors be shut? In the Appendix to the Gospel the scene on the Sea of Tiberias is stated to be the third appearance (xxi 14), according to which the Apostles remained in Jerusalem for over a week, saw the Lord twice, and then—Simon Peter goes a-fishing! Surely the only true deduction is that chapter xxi is a story constructed to explain away the death of the Beloved Disciple (xxi 23), not traditional reminiscence.

Of all this undoubtedly the strongest evidence to the historian for the Galilean theory comes from the two passages in Mark. The end of Mark indeed is lost; but, it may be asked, do we not know in substance the end of Mark? Is not the last chapter of Matthew based upon it? To discuss this question fully would take us too long from the immediate subject before us: I have only formulated the theory here in order to express my entire disagreement from it. In the story of the Passion Matthew follows Mark very closely, often word for word, and only differs from his source by inserting fresh matter from time to time, such as the dream of Pilate's wife and the story of the guards at the tomb. All this extra matter seems to me of a legendary and unhistorical character. And further, I see no reason to suppose that the copy of " Mark " which " Matthew " used did not end, like our oldest texts, at Mark xvi 8. The whole of Matt. xxviii 9–20, except the paragraph which finishes up the story of the guards (a story foreign to Mark), appears to me to be Matthew's peroration, added to round off by a suitable conclusion the mutilated narrative of the Second Gospel. It is usually said that Mark has only lost its last leaf: for this view there is really no evidence. In my opinion it is a more reasonable conjecture that Mark may have lost about a third of its original contents, and that the work once dealt with the period covered by Acts i–xii, including, for instance, the story of Rhoda, Mark's mother's maid. In any case I do not think we can infer what followed Mark xvi 8 from the contents of Matt. xxviii 9–20.

We are left then, when all is said and done, with two not easily reconcilable accounts: that of Mark, which seems to point to appearances of the Risen Lord in Galilee, and that of Luke, which definitely places the appearances near Jerusalem. Can we not do something to decide between these from the internal probabilities of the case? It may seem a bold thing to attempt, but I venture to think there are considerations which do deserve to be borne in mind.

In the first place, what we have to do is not merely to explain a legend, but to account for a fact, the fact that the historical result of the Passion and Crucifixion was that Peter and his companions settled down at Jerusalem. Galilee did not become a Christian country; so far as I know, there never were any Christians established in Galilee till the days when Christians were to be found in every corner of the Empire. As soon as we know anything about the earliest Christians we find them in Jerusalem and nowhere else.

Let us consider for a moment what would be the natural effect upon Peter or other disciples, if they returned to Galilee and saw their Lord there. The scene has been often sketched by imaginative writers. We are supposed to think of Peter returned to his old haunts by the Sea of Gennesaret, sad and disillusioned, and haunted by all the memories of the past. There one day, amid the old familiar surroundings, away from the hostile atmosphere of Jerusalem, he is convinced that he has seen his Lord and Master again. It was no ghost, he is certain of that ; the Lord had appeared to him alive !

This is all very well ; those who wish can fill in the details for themselves, rationalizing the visions more or less according to their taste and predilections. But we must go on to ask what would be the immediate effect upon Peter's comings and goings ; what would visions of the Risen Lord in Galilee make Peter do ? Surely, he would say, this is holy ground ; where I have seen the Lord once, there I may see Him again. The experience would have made him stay in Galilee.

If we are to invent visions in Galilee to explain to ourselves the course of events we cannot rest with mere visions, not even with visions accompanied by assurances, whether in the form of spoken words or intuitions, that the Lord Jesus was alive, and was or would be exalted soon to be with His Father in Heaven. We have to go on to invent a definite message to return to Jerusalem, something contrary to intuition, contrary to what was natural if Jesus had been seen in Galilee. It is not a question of believing an old tradition, but of inventing a new one, for the message to return is not included in the tradition. The documents that tell us of appearances in Galilee say nothing about returning to Jerusalem.

But what if Peter saw the Lord on the way, before he had got far from the Holy City? Would it not make him retrace his steps? Would he not take it first of all, in whatever form the vision may have been, as a sign that he ought not to leave Jerusalem? Where the Lord was seen, there He was, or somewhere near. This, and not the old haunts, was the holy ground, Jerusalem not Galilee. If the experience of Peter—and it was Peter's experience, no doubt, that was decisive—took place at Jerusalem, then we understand why Peter is found at Jerusalem as soon as we hear of him again. Otherwise it remains a riddle of which no reasonable explanation has ever been given.

For these reasons I think the Lucan view, that Peter and the little nucleus of believers never got more than a day's journey from

Jerusalem between the Crucifixion of Jesus and the Feast of Pentecost, is psychologically more probable than that which seems to be indicated in Mark and is actually set forth in Matthew, viz. that Peter and his companions did return to Galilee and there became convinced that their Lord had risen from the dead.

I have said "seems to be indicated in Mark," for after all it is not quite certain what Mark went on to narrate. It must continually be remembered that we have not only to deal with and explain the extant words of the Gospel but also the fact of Peter's return to Jerusalem. I do not wish to suggest that Peter did not intend to set out for Galilee; very likely he did start on his way. What I suggest is that he did not get very far. If he saw his Lord alive again while he was still in the neighbourhood of the city it would not only make him stay, abandoning his projected journey, but he would regard it as a kindly and gracious change of purpose. He who changed His settled and expressed practice for the sake of the Syrophenician woman might do so for Peter.

I cannot help sometimes wondering whether the well-known story of *Domine quo vadis?* where St. Peter flying from Rome meets Christ on the Appian Way and consequently turns back, may not have some historical foundation in what occurred on the first Easter Day near Jerusalem.

Moreover there is another point, which is perhaps worth some consideration. The story of the Last Supper and of Gethsemane in Mark surely bears the stamp of the eye-witness, of real reminiscence. I have given elsewhere my reasons for believing that even the chronological mistakes of this section are best explicable on the supposition that they contain the reminiscences, not of Peter, but of John Mark himself.[1] There are many things in this part of Mark's tale that only do not strike us as strange because we have heard them so often. The solemn vow of Jesus not to drink wine till He was drinking it new in the Kingdom of God (xiv 25)— that surely was not invented but remembered. And " Rise, let us be off : the traitor is close by ! " (xiv 42)—the Christian who first

[1] *J. Th. St.* xvii (1916), especially p. 296f.

wrote that down could have had no object but direct reminiscence. Is it not possible that xiv 28 (" I go before you into Galilee ") is real reminiscence of something that Mark heard, or rather overheard?

I should like once again to lay emphasis on the fact that there is no evidence in early times for any Galilean Christianity. Later wholly imaginative works like the *Epistola Apostolorum* (latter half of second century) may place revelations by the Lord to the Apostles in Galilee, just as *Pistis Sophia* places such revelations on the Mount of Olives, but this proves nothing for us: it only shows that the one work took the *mise en scène* of Matthew while the other took that of Luke. But of a community of Christians settled in Galilee there is, so far as I know, no trace.[1] In the Book of Acts we read of Christians in Damascus, of missions in Samaria, in the country about Lydda, on the sea coast, and in far-away lands, but the

[1] It does not quite appear where the little property was situated that was tilled by the grandsons of Jude, " brother of the Lord " (Euseb., *HE* iii 20). But even this story, which belongs to the times of Domitian (A.D. 81–95) does not speak of a Christian *Church* in Galilee.

only mention of Galilee (except in references to the career of Jesus) is that through the conversion of Paul "the church throughout all Judea and Galilee and Samaria had peace."[1]

It may be objected that I have passed over the witness of 1 Corinthians too lightly. Does not Paul say, in 1 Cor. xv 6, that Jesus appeared to above five hundred brethren at once? This indeed is a startling statement, startling because on the ordinary explanation this wonderful event has left no other trace, for the Christophany at the end of Matthew is expressly limited to the Eleven. As we all know, the famous list of appearances of the Risen Christ is given by St. Paul as that which he received. It must represent what was regarded by those who instructed him as the salient proofs that Christ had been raised up by God notwithstanding the Crucifixion. Now St. Paul almost identifies the Risen Christ and the Spirit: it would be remarkable if in his list he should make no mention of the great event of Pentecost. The inference seems to me obvious: the

[1] Acts ix 31.

appearance to five hundred brethren at once in 1 Cor. xv 6 is the same event that is related in the second chapter of Acts. The differences are very great, but so is the corresponding difference between the description of " speaking with tongues " by Paul and by Luke, though there can be little doubt that the same phenomenon is being described. As I understand the matter the simultaneous enthusiasm of the believers in Jerusalem on the Day of Pentecost was regarded by Paul as a Christophany, while in Acts the tale is told so as to suggest missionary effort in strange tones and dialects. Yet even so Luke manages to tell us the essential things, first that all the believers were seized together with religious ecstasy, but, secondly, that to Peter, while fully convinced of the reality of what his fellow-believers were experiencing, the enthusiasm took the form of courage to proclaim what they believed and eloquence to commend the astonishing story. In any case, different as the two statements are in 1 Corinthians and in Acts, the difficulty of equating them seems to me to be less than to suppose that the appearance to the five hundred took place in Galilee and was either unknown to Luke or that he did not think it worth while to insert it in his book.

These are my reasons for believing that the decisive "experiences" of St. Peter, which convinced him that his Lord was risen indeed, occurred at or near Jerusalem. I am unable therefore to agree with the statement in *Beginnings*, i 303, that there is " the strongest probability that Luke has omitted or transformed the story of the disciples in Galilee and their return to Jerusalem," and the corresponding footnote loses its force, which says: ·" This is the measure of the caution with which statements in the early part of Acts must be received, and the justification for a free criticism." Yes, indeed; if in recounting to Theophilus the things most certainly believed among Christians Luke has suppressed the sojourn of Peter and his companions in the north during which they became convinced that Christ was risen, and has substituted for it a tale of their remaining during this period at Jerusalem, then Acts ceases to deserve to be regarded as an historical document. But, as I have attempted to explain, I think this hypothesis of a short stay in Galilee, followed by a return to Jerusalem, raises more difficulties than it explains. In the most general way, then, the tale at the beginning of Acts keeps within the lines of history. It does not lose at the start the right to be taken as a guide to the course of events, while on the other hand those documents, such as the peroration of the Gospel of Matthew and the *Epistola Apostolorum*, which do set forth the Galilean theory, have no claim to be called historical.

In conclusion, there is one aspect of the Lucan account of the Risen Christ that is generally overlooked. It is purely negative, but it seems to me to supply a reason for believing not only in the literary skill, but also in the discretion and *bona fides* of our guide. Strange as it seems to us, a good many early Christians felt no scruple in making the Risen Christ a mouthpiece for their views. The whole of the Gnostic book, *Pistis Sophia*, is presented as a revelation made to the disciples by Jesus after the Resurrection. The Apocalypse of Peter consists of a revelation made to Peter and his companions by the Risen Jesus about the fate of righteous and wicked souls after death: this is the essence of the work, and the Gospel of Peter, found in close connexion with it, seems to be chiefly intended as an Introduction to these apocryphal (if edifying) revelations. These, you may say, are the work of heretics; but Catholic writers are equally bold. The newly-discovered *Epistola Apostolorum* appears to be an orthodox anti-Gnostic work, dating from the second half of the second century: this relates a long revelation to the Apostles by the Risen Lord. The climax is reached, no doubt, by the *Testamentum Domini*, where again it is the Risen Lord who speaks, and gives the Apostles directions not only for the conduct of public worship, but even about the pattern for planning churches.

Contrast all this with the post-resurrectional teaching of the Lord Jesus as given in Luke xxiv and Acts i. The writer indeed so presents his material as to make the figure of Jesus live and move far more naturally than in any of the works I have just named. How gracious is the story of the Two Disciples and their walk to Emmaus! We seem to see Jesus accompanying them and joining in their troubled and anxious talk. But no fresh revelation is recorded by Luke. "The Christ must suffer these things and then enter into His glory"—this is no more than Luke xviii 31 and many similar verses. "Beginning from Moses and all the prophets he expounded unto them in all the Scriptures the things concerning Himself"—yes, and Luke does not even think proper to name one single proof-text. Luke xxiv 38, 39, only mean "It was the real Jesus, not a ghost," and *ver.* 41 is the same. *Ver.* 49 is the nearest to a real fresh Saying; it tells the witnesses to stay in Jerusalem till further developments occur. That, as I have argued, would have been the result of an appearance of Jesus in, or near Jerusalem, without any further word, so that this Saying springs of itself from the historical situation there portrayed. In Acts i, again, the only fresh saying is *ver.* 7, and so far from being a fresh revelation it is a refusal to give one. As it stands it is a direct parallel to Luke xvii 20 and to Mark xiii 32—no one can tell when the End will come, sufficient for the day is the evil thereof, and the Christian must rest content with the certainty that the supply of supernatural grace will suffice to carry him through the interim.

It is a meagre crop, compared with the rich harvest of secret doctrine or prophecy that so many other Christian documents did not hesitate to supply. Is it, I ask, not a fair measure of the Lucan intellectual honesty, of his scientific scruple as an historian? He could have supplied so much more, if he had thought it right. The writer who planned the speeches in Acts could easily have extemporized instructions to Peter about the admission of Gentiles into the Church, to name but one among the pressing questions of the Apostolic Age. It is only right that we should remember this abstention when we come to consider what sort of weight should be assigned to the historical statements in Acts.

The argument here presented is not a plea to accept the narrative of Acts as either an accurate or a complete account of the earliest days of the Christian Church. "Luke" is a conscious artist who selects and arranges his material to produce the impression he desires to convey, not a mere chronicler who heaps up material. But this impression was, in my opinion, that which he had formed from his study of the material with which he was acquainted. In particular, I think we ought not to come to the Book of Acts with a prejudice against it because it does not tell us of a " Galilean Period " in which the nucleus of the Church was formed, for the theory that such a period ever existed raises insuperable difficulties and makes the subsequent course of events inexplicable.

LECTURE III

THE narrative of Acts tells us how the Christian Society started at Jerusalem, gradually extended itself by missions to other parts of the Land of Israel—though about Galilee a significant silence is maintained—and then, as the indirect result of a persecution caused by the opposition to the teaching of Stephen, the Gospel is carried to Antioch and begins to make its way among a non-Jewish population.

In the previous Lecture I have attempted to show that the prejudices of some modern scholars against the main outline of the tale in the opening scenes are unfounded. The modest claim of the writer to be an historian, formulated in the Preface to the Third Gospel, is a just one. But it cannot be denied that his account of the early days is extremely sketchy. "Sir, I could wish for more," said Samuel Johnson to Boswell about the evidences of Christianity in general; it may well be echoed about the narrative of Acts i–xii in particular.

Acts xii ends with the death of Herod Agrippa; this took place in A.D. 44. The latest possible date for the Crucifixion is A.D. 35, and most investigators put it five or six years earlier. The first twelve chapters of Acts, therefore, cover a period of something between nine and fifteen years. But the events related, as they stand, belong to not more than thirty separate days, and there is no definite scheme of chronology, or indication where the gaps in the continuous narrative really occur. Work on such a scale may be historical in character, it may create a sound historical impression, but it is a sketch, not a history. I have ventured sometimes to label these chapters of Acts as " Scenes from Early Days,"[1] for they are detached vignettes, not a continuous panorama.

It must be acknowledged that one reason for this paucity of description may have been that there was little to describe. The Believers doubtless attracted little attention,

[1] See *Beginnings*, ii 433.

at least after the excitement of the first Pentecost died down. No doubt their main attitude was one of waiting, patient or impatient according to temperament. They continued—or many of them did—with Peter and the other Apostles, " in the breaking of bread and the prayers "; they had all things in common and lived on the realized capital of the richer ones among them. These things are duly chronicled by Luke. But how interested we should be if we could hear their discussions when the anniversary of the Passover came round, when no doubt the Lord was confidently expected—and when He still delayed! Then again, when according both to Josephus and to Philo the Jewish people were in an agony of excitement at the intention of the Emperor Caligula to set up his image in the Temple, what did the Believers think of it? Did it make them remember that the Lord Jesus had Himself used the words of Daniel and spoken of the "abomination of desolation" as a sign of the End? Perhaps so, and perhaps therefore this incident has left its traces on the Gospels. But not a word of it can be found in the vignettes of Acts.

Barnabas is an interesting personality, of whom we would gladly know more, not only before he comes upon the scene in Acts and after he has left it, but also as to his opinions and development during the time we do hear something of him.

With Stephen there is introduced a fresh element. "Jesus this Nazarene will destroy this Place—the Temple at Jerusalem —and change the way of life that Moses delivered to us": this is said to have been the accusation against him (Acts vi 14), and indeed such a doctrine was a more serious crime against the Jewish State than that of Caligula. The accusation, as reported in Acts, is couched in the future tense. So far as it goes it might be nothing more than a forecast of the future, in the Age to Come. But the fact of Stephen's lawless execution shows the passions that he roused; there must have been something immediate and practical in his attitude to the whole religious system to have excited such opposition. One special point of interest suggests itself to me as I read the story of Stephen. What is the connexion between Stephen's teaching about the Temple and the sacrificial worship generally, and the " Cleansing of the Temple " by our Lord? The early Believers, according to Acts, were continually in the Temple, but they are said to have used it for prayer and to have " broken their bread " at home. Did they habitually offer sacrifices still? On occasion, yes; from time to time some of them would make a religious vow, the completion of which would mean a sacrifice or sacrificial dues (Acts xxi 24). But did they keep the Passover year after year? We do not know; but as I pointed out in the preceding Lecture, the man who came to be the hero and the recognized head of the community practically contracted himself out of the sacrificial system by becoming an ascetic and a vegetarian.

It is easier to ask these questions than to find answers.

The martyrdom of Stephen dispersed the members of his party, some of whom betook themselves to Antioch, with most important after-results (Acts xi 19ff), for they founded Gentile Christianity and it is at Antioch that the Believers first get the new name of Christians. It is notable that " the Apostles," i.e. Peter and his friends, remained undisturbed at Jerusalem. Somewhat later, in the days of Herod Agrippa, i.e. between A.D. 41 and 44, James the brother of John is executed and it pleases " the Jews " (Acts xii 3), by which I suppose our historian means popular feeling in Jerusalem. Peter also is arrested and was intended for execution, but manages to escape. The story as told is miraculous, and indeed Peter and the anxious party gathered at the house of the mother of John surnamed Mark may have been ignorant of the methods by which the guards remained asleep when the prison-gate was opened. But the story gives me the impression that some human sympathizer was at work, who had drugged the guards and bribed the turnkey. At any rate, if it really was the Angel of the Lord it seems rather hard upon the unfortunate guards of Peter that they should have been executed by Herod in his stead.[1] I prefer to believe that Peter's escape was contrived by human means.

Be this as it may, we seem to see suggested by these tales in Acts three types of Christians who emerge in the early stage before St. Paul. They are marked by the different attitude of the populace of Jerusalem towards them. To Stephen and his party Jerusalem is hostile; as soon as they come into public view their leader is killed and his friends dispersed. At the other end is James the Just, the Brother of the Lord, who is first mentioned in Acts by name and as a leader in this story of Peter's escape (ver. 17). No popular outbreak against the Nazarenes seems to touch him: he becomes, we do not know by what stages, the unquestioned head of the Believers in the Holy City and yet remains in favour with all the people. Between these extremes comes Peter: he had been unaffected by the persecution of Stephen, but later on he is singled out, because the would-be orthodox King Herod thinks he will be a popular

[1] Acts xii 19.

victim. Even apart from the Pauline Epistles and the story of Cornelius we should infer that Peter himself had become a "liberal," that at least he was suspected, and suspected with justice, of a tendency to incline to the side of Stephen.

The story of Cornelius, which comes in Acts between the tales of Stephen and of Peter's imprisonment, is in detail somewhat unsatisfactory for the modern historian. The writer of Acts is too obviously pleased with it. He has too obviously made it the occasion of speech-writing, in the phrasing of which if not in the whole subject-matter it is only too easy to see the hand of the literary artist and not very easy to see anything else. But the incident itself seems to me to fit the character of Peter and his subsequent conduct too well to be mere invention. The influence of F. C. Baur is still so strong that it makes us unreasonably suspicious of any testimony to the liberalism of Peter, but (to quote once again the well-considered remark of the Editors of *Beginnings*) it is one of the mistakes of the Tübingen School that it did not recognize that Peter, not only in the Acts but also in the Pauline Epistles, is on the Hellenistic not the Hebrew side.[1]

So we see the stage gradually prepared for the career of Paul, the converted Pharisee. He had been an opponent of Stephen, was "consenting to his death," and was on an errand of persecution when, as he phrases it, "God revealed His Son in me!" Thanks to his Letters we can get to know the mind of Paul very well: what we do not know in detail are the opinions of Saul of Tarsus. He was a Pharisee, one who observed the Law strictly. He had studied under Gamaliel; but, as C. G. Montefiore has reminded us, we do not know what proficiency he acquired in the specifically Rabbinic lore—for instance, I do not think he has anywhere quoted or adapted any known utterance of Gamaliel. Mr. Montefiore's *caveat* is timely, for Christians have been too apt to regard St. Paul as having attained the very pinnacle of Jewish learning. This, no doubt, is a mistake. But his lore

[1] *Beginnings*, i 312.

was surely considerable, as may be seen, e.g. from Dr. H. St. J. Thackeray's work on the subject.[1]

In any case the Jewish culture is the only culture visible in St. Paul's Epistles. I mean, of course, what may be described as school-culture. Neither Greek literature, nor Stoic philosophy, nor—as I think—anything of current Greek religious ideas, is to be found in the Letters of Paul, beyond what may be regarded as the common property of everyone to whom the common Greek of the Levant was a native language. The acquaintance he shows with the " Mystery-religions " and their terminology seems to me exactly comparable to the acquaintance shown by many clergymen to-day with Evolution, who nevertheless have neither been trained in a laboratory nor read the *Origin of Species*. On the other hand his Jewish lore is certainly there: he brings it in even

[1] To give but one instance. St. Paul is the only Christian writer in whose Biblical quotations the influence of the Aramaic Targums can be traced, or rather of the artificial exegesis which is known to us from Jewish sources through the Targums. The most notable instance is Eph. iv 8f, but the influence can be traced elsewhere.

in writing to Galatians who were heathen before they were Christians. And both in quantity and in depth it is more than could have been derived from mere untaught study of the Scriptures; it is a real school-culture, the argumentation of an educated man.

There is one illustration of this, so important in itself that it is worthy of special notice in passing. The doctrine of the New Birth of the Christian in baptism is a well-established article of orthodox belief. It finds clear support in the New Testament from the Gospel of John and the Epistle known as 1 Peter. But this conception is one of the leading ideas in the Mystery-religions; *renatus in aeternum* is not a Christian but a pagan formula, connected with the dreadful ceremony of the Taurobolium. Consequently it has been suggested that the very idea of the New Birth is one of the things which Christian thought has adopted from heathen religion.

It is therefore of great importance to notice that the idea of the New Birth is absent from the writings of St. Paul. What corresponds to it is a different idea, viz. that of the New Creation. This is a quite different idea: the baptized convert is not thought of as a child, but as one miraculously changed into a new and full-grown estate. It is congruous with all the rest of St. Paul's thinking; it involves miracle, but not magic. Now this peculiar phrase is not characteristic of the heathen mysteries, but it is found in Rabbinical theology. When God said to Abraham " I will make thee a great nation," this was explained to be not natural or inherent; it was a fresh act of God, a "new creation."[1] Very likely St. Paul's phraseology may have at once suggested to his heathen converts the corresponding heathen idea, but it is clear that in this crucial instance " the Hellenization of the Gospel " is not due to St. Paul himself.

But however learned Paul may have been, and whatever remnants of the lore and exegetical methods of Rabbinism he may have continued to use, his fundamental ideas

[1] See Schöttgen, i 704 (on Gal. vi 15). He quotes, among other instances, *Bereshith rabba*, §39.

were utterly opposed to popular Judaism. He refused to regard himself as a rebel, and I fancy that his ordinary personal habits and predilections were those of a respectable Jew. But in theory he was an ethical anarchist, and the net result of his announcement of the Gospel in heathen lands was that many Gentiles claimed to be full members of the Church, who had never been circumcised and had no intention of ordering their life in accordance with the Law of Moses—or indeed, so far as the older Jewish Believers could make out, in accordance with any rules whatever. These older Believers had every reason to be alarmed. In the famous Conference, which we shall have to consider, Peter is said to have said something about the yoke of ordinances which even born Jews had found burdensome. This is a reasonable, common-sense plea coming from a Jew living in a Gentile society, and is doubly so if applied to a Gentile convert. But there is nothing about this in Paul's Letters. There is nothing at all about the "burdensomeness" or the "triviality" of the Law. Paul delighted in it after the inner man, in his better moments, when he was wishing to do God's will. His trouble was that he did not always *wish* to do God's will. He was not seeking a new style of living but motives for wishing to live well, and his complaint against the Law is that it did not help him to wish to live well. When St. Paul is talking about the Law, he is hardly ever thinking of ceremonies and tithes and phylacteries: he is thinking about the Ten Commandments. When he says "All things are allowable," he really means it. There is a "but," of course, there always is; only he was trying to make it an inner tendency, not an external compulsion. It is this remarkable psychological thinking that makes his Letters, when properly understood, so vivid and interesting to-day, so that familiar as they are they still sound in parts rather dangerous, and they must have sounded flamingly dangerous to the Believers in Jerusalem. Probably indeed they had never read the Letters themselves, but only heard garbled accounts of Paul's talk. No wonder there was a demand for a minimum of common decency and behaviour from these Gentile newcomers, if they were to be received as fellow-worshippers.

In Acts xv we read that a Conference was held at Jerusalem, that an Agreement was reached which in effect was a victory for the inclusive, liberal view, but that a minimum of decent ethical observance was insisted on, which was embodied in a Decree or Circular Letter, which is quoted in full in Acts xv 23–29.

Every statement in the above sentences is a subject of controversy, and only a few points can be touched upon here. The most serious difficulty is to fit an acceptance of the Decree with the ethical system championed by S. Paul, for whereas most of the other difficulties come from our comparative ignorance, this comes from the express statements of the Apostle himself. I believe that there is a way of reconciliation, but it involves a particular view of the date and purport of almost all the earlier Epistles. I shall therefore come to these considerations last, after considering the Decree itself.

CHRISTIAN BEGINNINGS 113

Is the Decree altogether a fiction, invented by Luke? This view indeed has been held, but it seems to me quite untenable. I should be fully prepared to find that Luke had rewritten it. If a copy of the original turned up in some ruin or grave I should not be surprised to find that it was couched in language that resembled a page of Mark rather than what we read in Acts. But I should expect the substance to be the same, for I do not think we have any reason to suspect the author of Acts of real bad faith. We are not, however, reduced to such general considerations. The writer of the Book of Revelation, himself in touch with Jewish Christianity if not actually a Jewish Christian, writing to the Church of Thyatira, reproves the lax ethical teaching current there, but tells those who have not received it " I put upon you no other burden." [1] This at once suggests the words of the Apostolical Decree (Acts xv 28). But this is not all. What are the teachings of the false prophetess whom the Apocalyptist calls " Jezabel "? Why, he says that she teaches the servants

[1] Rev. ii 24, οὐ βάλλω ἐφ' ὑμᾶσ ἄλλο βάρcσ.

of God to commit fornication and to eat things offered to idols (πορνεῦσαι καὶ φαγεῖν εἰδωλόθυτα)! We do not quite know what is intended by this; probably the lady would have disclaimed these terms. As they stand, however, they are the two most important of the four practices condemned by name in the Decree. I think it is impossible to avoid regarding this passage in the Apocalypse otherwise than as a direct reference to the Decree. And, as it is most improbable that the writer derived his knowledge of it from Acts itself, it follows that the author of Acts did not invent the Decree.

What does the Decree mean? Is it a food-law, or a moral injunction? As we all know, there is here an important " various reading." "Things strangled" are omitted by Codex Bezae and the " Western " authorities generally, and the same authorities mostly add to the prohibitions, now reduced to three, a negative form of the " Golden Rule." By this means the food law is turned into a moral catechism. "Things offered to idols" are then understood to mean idolatry in general, " blood " to mean murder, and " fornication " all breaches of the seventh commandment.

It is a very nice question. The best defence of the theory that the Decree is a moral catechism is Lake's, in *The Earlier Epp. of St. Paul*, pp. 48-60. Lake there defends a text like Tertullian's, which omits both καὶ πνικτῶν and the negative form of the Golden Rule. But on the whole I think that the ordinary Alexandrian text, which must be regarded as being at least partly a food-law, raises the fewest difficulties. Paul's complaint against Peter in Gal. ii 12 was that after the arrival of certain strict believers from Jerusalem he would no longer *eat* with the Gentile Christians. And as we may at least suppose that the writer of Acts wrote from a generally consistent point of view it is appropriate to observe that what offended the stricter Jerusalemite believers in Acts xi 3 was not that Peter had baptized Cornelius, but that he had eaten with him.

There is one further consideration. What was the immediate use of this food-law for Gentile Christians ? Not, I think, to ensure their own salvation, now or hereafter, but to ensure that Jewish believers who might be accepting their hospitality would not be offended or scandalized. It was the terms of inter-communion ; and on this very subject what St. Paul says is, " Do not scandalize your more scrupulous fellow-believer with the food which you believe you may eat and he believes he may not eat " (Rom. xiv 20, 21). Anyone who followed St. Paul's advice would automatically obey the Apostolic Decree.

We have thus come to what is after all the most important part of the question. If the substance of the Decree be genuine, how can we interpret the Letters of Paul ? In attempting an answer to this I shall start from the Decree, arranging and explaining the several Letters with reference to it. Then at the end we shall see if the result is generally harmonious.

Galatians. The most natural interpretation of the biographical statements in Galatians i and ii is that they were written before the " Council " at Jerusalem. This implies what is called the South-Galatian theory, which means in effect that the persons addressed are the Christians of Antioch in Pisidia and of Derbe and Lystra in Lycaonia, about whom we read in Acts xiii and xiv. The visit to Jerusalem described by Paul in Gal. ii. 1-10 corresponds then to Acts xi 30, not to Acts xv. The difficulties in this view, as I understand it, are consequential: in itself, so far as Acts and Galatians alone are concerned it seems a most attractive solution. The Letter, so we must think, will have been originally penned at the height of the dispute about circumcision, and was written, probably when Paul was actually on his way to Jerusalem, to encourage the Pisidian and Lycaonian converts to stand firm, whatever the Jewish-Christian conservatives might demand from them as of right. Incidentally it may be observed that the earlier Galatians is dated, the easier it is to explain the phrase in ii 8, which calls Peter an Apostle of the Circumcision, for the episode of Cornelius, however historical in itself, is narrated in Acts as quite an exceptional event, outside the usual sphere of Peter's activity. Further, the circumcision of Titus by Paul—for who can doubt that it was the knife which really did circumcise Titus that has cut the syntax of Gal. ii 3–5 to pieces?—the circumcision of Titus is far more likely to have been decided on by Paul at the earlier period, when nothing was stabilized and individual concessions may have been graceful and wise, than at the very moment when Paul is fighting with all his powers against compelling Gentiles to submit to circumcision. If this early date be not accepted I do not see how Galatians can be reconciled with Acts. If the conference at Jerusalem was anything in the least like what we read in Acts xv, then Gal. ii 1–10 is a misleading account of it, and if Gal. ii 1–10 refers to Acts xi 30, but was written after the conference of Acts xv took place, then we cannot acquit St. Paul of a wilful and inexcusable suppression of material facts, facts which nevertheless would be fully in the hands of all his adversaries. But with the earlier date for Galatians all these serious difficulties disappear.

1 *and 2 Corinthians.* The group of Letters which we know as 1 and 2 Corinthians were written about A.D. 55, some five years after the Conference at Jerusalem, and the date we have assigned to Galatians. These years had witnessed great developments. The Gospel had been carried from Asia to Europe, wholly new classes of converts had been reached. The numbers of the Gentile Christians were now considerable: it is impossible to estimate the number in figures, but I suppose that whereas at the Conference at Jerusalem they may have been reckoned by dozens, at the time 1 Corinthians was being written they would have been reckoned by hundreds. In correspondence with this fact we notice that the position of the Gentiles is now assured. The only reference to circumcision in either Epistle is 1 Cor. vii 18, 19, where it seems to be brought in less for its own sake than as affording an analogy for the question of marriage or celibacy. St. Paul has plenty of opponents of course, but they do not seem to be exclusively or even mainly Jewish. "He is afraid, or has no authority, to ask for our financial support,"

or "he is not so full of the Spirit as others," or "his Letters are weighty and powerful, but his bodily presence is weak and his speech contemptible"—these seem to be the things that the adversaries were saying. There was no special reason why he should refer back to the rulings of the Conference four or five years ago. The case is quite different from that of the Galatian Epistle, in which he is professing to give a more or less connected statement of his relations with the heads of the Jerusalem Church.

All the same, it is remarkable how much of 1 Corinthians is taken up with questions concerning "things offered to idols," and "fornication." The latter subject occupies all chap. v, also vi 12–20, and all vii; the former all chap. viii and x 19–32. Does Paul in these passages agree with the Decree? Does he show himself loyal to his engagements? These questions are sometimes asked, but I do not think they admit of an answer, because they are not the right questions to ask. In the first place the Decree as given in Acts is not a treaty between St. Paul and St. James. We are not even told that Paul consented to it. It does not appear indeed that his consent was asked. As it stands it does no more than state the terms upon which the authorities at Jerusalem were willing to eat the food of Gentile believers, i.e. to accept their manner of life as decent and seemly. After all, the general purport of the Decree is that the "Judaizers" had had no commission from the responsible folk at Jerusalem. Certain practices at the end are reprobated, but the intention of the document is obviously to allow most of what the Judaizers had represented as culpably lax.

But did Paul not approve of it? I imagine that he thought the requirements very sensible and reasonable, very suitable as a general guide to that large class of persons whom he speaks of as "weak." Rather than that such persons should suffer injury to their religious life he was prepared to do without meat and wine altogether. What he was not prepared to admit was that any rule was of obligation in itself, i.e. as binding between God and himself *qua* rule. If the thing was right in itself you ought to wish to do it, otherwise mere outward conformity was real rebellion. But on the other hand there is no reason why you should not obey the Law if you wanted to do so. And clearly, in a great many points, Paul's wishes were in conformity with the Law. He was convinced, obviously, that the Seventh Commandment was a good rule for human society, he was enthusiastically convinced that he was a member of Christ and it seemed to him shocking that a member of Christ should be ".joined to a harlot" (1 Cor. vi 15). On this question, therefore, there was no opposition between him and the terms of the Decree. But what Paul desired was to persuade his disciples to obey the Decree for the same reasons that influenced him. The motive was everything to him: "whatsoever is not of faith is sin."

That is the high Paulinist doctrine. What, however, is also clear is that (like most theoretical anarchists) he did not always live up to it. In other moods Paul issues his own Decrees, and I do not find them always convincing. The whole of Christendom, so far as I know, has adopted his un-Jewish rule that men shall pray with their heads uncovered. It may be a good rule, but it does not seem to me so inevitably obvious as it seemed to Paul. And what did Louis XIV or John Milton or John Bunyan (who all had what we should call long hair) think of 1 Cor. xi 14? What would Paul have said if these men had told him that cropping their hair might have indeed a show of wisdom in will-worship and humility and severity to the body, but was not of any value or honour against the indulgence of the flesh?[1] My point is, that St. Paul did not mind issuing ordinances on occasion. If therefore the recommendations in the Apostolical Decree happened to be such as in St. Paul's eyes "nature itself teaches" (1 Cor. xi 14), then I do not think he would have felt it inconsistent with "his" gospel to recommend them, even to enforce them. As I have said above, a good deal of 1 Corinthians is actually occupied with the two most important of the four recommendations of the Decree. And I imagine that Paul considered that the

[1] See Col. ii 23.

teaching of 1 Cor. viii was directly in accordance with it. The Decree said "Gentile Christians are not to eat things offered to idols," obviously therefore some Christians think this practice in itself wrong. Paul says: Intelligent Christians know that idols are nothing and that all things are lawful to eat. But some weaker brethren think this food is forbidden—if they think so, it *is* forbidden to them. If then they see you at a heathen feast, they will be emboldened to eat this food themselves, which to them is a sin. Therefore," he concludes, " do not eat this food yourselves for the sake of the conscience of others." In other words, the recommendation of Paul is the recommendation of the Decree: what is different is the ethical theory on which the recommendation is based.

St. Paul does not touch in 1 Corinthians or elsewhere upon "blood," or "things strangled," in connexion with food. It does not seem to be quite certain what these words mean in practice. Obviously the significance or non-significance of Paul's silence in this matter depends upon whether the

Corinthians were in the habit of eating αἷμα or πνικτά within the meaning of the Decree. How did they kill chickens at Corinth in the first century A.D.? Did they wring their necks or cut their heads off? Or did they practise the modern way? I have made some inquiries on this subject from my classical friends, but have not got much light. Yet it is obvious that until we know what went on in the Corinthian kitchens and back-yards of those days we are not in a position to judge St. Paul on this head. Perhaps he himself " asked no questions, for conscience' sake" (1 Cor. x 27).

Romans. It is clear that Rom. xv 19–29 was written shortly before Paul went up to Jerusalem for the last time, bearing with him the collection he had made from the Gentile Churches for the " poor among the saints " there. With this goes the long list of greetings in chap. xvi. It may surprise us that Paul had so large an acquaintance in Rome; in fact it has been suggested that this is a Postscript addressed elsewhere, e.g. Ephesus. For this there is no solid evidence: what is certain is that if the list be really Roman its size shows us that it comes late in the Apostle's career.

On the other hand, the rest of the Epistle is a theological treatise with no personal and local allusions, and both in style and subject-matter it is very closely allied to Galatians. It is very difficult to think of St. Paul beginning with Galatians, then going on to develop the style seen in 2 Cor. iv and v, then going back to Romans, and then onward once more to the Epistles of the captivity. Now in the matter of the date of Romans textual criticism really does come to the aid of literary and historical study, for the Epistle has been transmitted in two forms. There is an admirable discussion of the subject in Lake's *Earlier Epistles* (see esp. pp. 348, 362f.), the upshot of which is that both forms are Pauline. The earlier form, consisting of Rom i–xiv (with or without the great Doxology, xvi 25–27) was a circular letter or treatise, contemporary with Galatians: in this form no place-name was inserted in i 7 and 15. A copy of this circular letter, containing as it does St. Paul's theory of Law and Grace, the mission of Israel, and the bearing of the theory on Christian ethics, was sent by him to Rome when he was on his way to Jerusalem. The immediate occasion was to introduce Phœbe (xvi 1), who was no doubt the bearer of the Letter, to the Roman Christians.

The only thing I have to add to Professor Lake's argument is to remark that Rom. xv 1–13 seems to me exactly the sort of writing that we should expect in these circumstances. Rom. xiv 23 indeed is a real conclusion: nothing but a Doxology is really in place after it. But in the longer form Paul wanted to lead up to his personal statements in xv 19ff, so he continues his own argument for a sentence or two, and then quotes a few texts from the Prophets. Those of us who are writers, who have had occasion to adapt an address or a lecture designed for one audience to suit another, will at various times have been engaged on a similar task. No doubt Rom. xv 1–13 is not Paul at his best; it is a weld, a join, an adaptation. But those who have themselves attempted the same sort of work will be the last to be surprised at its defects.

In Rom. xiv we have the same doctrine about food-laws in general that is given in 1 Cor. viii with reference to " things offered to idols." We, the intelligent believers, should meet the scrupulous half-way by giving them no offence, while cherishing our internal freedon before God (xiv 22). It all seems to me completely in accordance with the Apostolical Decree, so far as the course of action recommended is concerned. And the Decree is only concerned with outward practices, not with religious theory.

1 *and* 2 *Thessalonians.* The scheme set out in the above paragraphs is, as I think, a satisfactory account of the relation of the four great Epistles of Paul to the Decree given in Acts. And, further, the order suggested, viz. Galatians and Romans (ed. 1), followed by 1 and 2 Corinthians, and then Romans (ed. 2), while arrived at from considerations connected with the Decree is found to be harmonious with the general style and tendencies of the Epistles themselves. But how on this scheme are we to explain the Thessalonian Epistles? Their date is obvious from 1 Thess. iii 1, 6: it must be while

Paul is still at Athens, or perhaps on his first arrival at Corinth, i.e. only a few months after the Conference at Jerusalem. There is in these Letters no allusion to the Decree, unless a warning in 1 Thess iv 2f against fornication be regarded as such, but this may be explained on the ground that the circumstances did not call for any allusion to it. The difficulty is that the Letters, while full of genuinely Pauline ideas and expressions, are as wholes much weaker in style than the four great Letters. If Paul had written Galatians six months before and had already composed the treatise that we know as Rom. i.-xiv, is it conceivable that he would produce anything like 1 Thessalonians? And the same argument applies to 2 Thessalonians with even greater force.

Should we be impressed with this line of argument and regard the Thessalonian Letters as spurious we are confronted with a curious state of things. There was plenty of Pseudepigraphical writing in late-Judaism and among the early Christians, but the unauthentic document continually betrays itself by marks of a later date. Exactly the reverse is the case with the Thessalonian Letters. If the indications of the ostensible date were not so precise we should have very little difficulty in regarding them as works of Paul's earliest Christian period; for instance, when he was working under Barnabas at Antioch. There is no better summary of the earliest Christian creed than 1 Thess. i 9, 10. The whole outlook, indeed, is what might be described as pre-Pauline. Again, the details of the eschatological expectations are much more naïve than what we get in the other Epistles, e.g. in 1 Cor. xv: the Man of Sin and the Mystery of Lawlessness (2 Thess. ii 3, 7) never appear again. And I think it not unfair to note that nowhere else in the Pauline Corpus do we find such hard words against the Jewish nation in general as in 1 Thess. ii 14-16. Yet we have reason to believe that at this very time Paul was still cherishing a hope of the final conversion of his much-beloved fellow-countrymen, and had recently expressed his hope in Rom. ix-xi.

In a word, the Thessalonian Epistles are Pauline but not Paul's own, yet they cannot have been written at a later date. Is there any way of satisfying all these indications? I venture to think that there is.

The solution I suggest is that they are, as they profess to be, the Letters of Paul and Silvanus and Timothy, and that this means that whoever was the scribe they were drafted by Silvanus, better known to us by his Jewish name Silas.

Who *wrote* the Epistles of St. Paul? Galatians we know was written out by Paul himself. A certain Tertius wrote the long form of Romans (xvi 22). Timothy wrote 2 Corinthians, Philippians, Colossians, and Philemon. Sosthenes is named with Paul at the beginning of 1 Corinthians. No name is associated with the Apostle for Ephesians: Tychicus is mentioned in vi 21, but there is nothing to suggest that he was the scribe. Of these names Tertius was obviously of no importance, and I do not doubt that Timothy did what he was told to do and no more. Of the hand of Sosthenes I wish we did know more: in some ways 1 Corinthians is the best arranged of all the Letters, and part of this may be due to the secretary. But Silvanus, called in Acts Silas, was in his day a much more important person than either of these. He was an old believer of Jerusalem, one of " the chief men among the brethren " and a " prophet " (Acts xv 22, 32). But though he came from the very stronghold of Jewish Christianity he attached himself to Paul, and Paul chose him for a travelling companion when Barnabas failed. Silas (or Sileas) is a known Jewish name (*Sh'ilā*), meaning " Little Saul ": it is likely therefore that like Paul he was a Benjamite, which may have helped to cement the friendship of the two men.

When therefore we read " Paul and Silvanus " it is not by any means to be assumed that the second name means little or nothing for the contents. My suggestion, therefore, is that both Letters were drafted by Silvanus-Silas, that they were read to Paul, who approved them and added 1 Thess. ii 18 and 2 Thess. iii 17 with his own hand. No doubt he made other suggestions elsewhere, but the terms of the Postscript added in Paul's autograph suggest that he is not

CHRISTIAN BEGINNINGS 133

wholly responsible for all the rest.[1] The Letters were approved by Paul, but the structure, the drafting, and some of the ideas are not his. A man will cordially approve a thing which would have been differently worded if he had composed it himself.

All the rest of what has been written about these two Letters may stand. Very likely 2 Thessalonians is, as Harnack suggests, directed to the Jewish part of the Thessalonian community. What is gained by my hypothesis is an easy explanation both of their likeness and unlikeness to the rest of the Pauline Letters. Above all, the authorship of Silas explains the archaic features of Thessalonians; the two Letters are what they read like, a monument of not quite the earliest stage of Jerusalemite Christianity. If I may hazard a final guess, I should say that Silas had heard St. Stephen gladly.

To sum up, the conclusion here reached is that there is little reason to doubt the historicity of the substance of the Apostolic

---

[1] Somewhat similar Postscripts are added at 1 Cor. xvi 21, Col. iv 18, but what in these instances is given as a greeting appears as a sort of guarantee in 2 Thess. iii 17.

Decree given in Acts xv. It was a law regulating the diet and social behaviour that Gentile Christians must adopt if Jewish Christians were to feel free to eat with them. As a rule of life it was such as St. Paul would approve, or at least be quite ready to comply with, so long as it was understood by intelligent Christians to be a concession to the scruples of others, not a positive Divine ordinance. And further, this view helps us to determine with certainty the order of the composition of the earlier Pauline Epistles.

There is one point I want to lay stress on before we leave the controversy about the admission of the Gentiles. Of all the questions that agitated the early Christians this is the one we know most about, for we hear something from both sides, and our documents include first-hand authorities like the Letters of Paul. We learn that the controversy was really fierce, and echoes of it are traceable for a long time after the struggle had ended. Moreover it was concerned with great principles, indeed with the very constitution of the Christian Society.

Now there is a school of critical interpretation of ancient documents which tends to discredit the statements of ancient historical writers as evidence for the sayings or doings they profess to relate, while at the same time these statements are regarded as valuable historical material for circumstances contemporary with the writers themselves. The instance of this often perverse method which I have in mind is to be found in *Beginnings*, vol. i, pp. 314-318, where the Editors discredit the reports of the missionary addresses of Jesus to the Twelve and to the Seventy-two as historical utterances of Jesus, while at the same time they attempt to use them as reflecting the opinions of various branches of more lax or more scrupulous Jewish Christians during the controversy about the admission of Gentiles.

I do not think the attempt is very successful. I am not holding a brief for the inerrancy of the Gospels. Words have doubtless been ascribed to Jesus which He never uttered. I own that I regard Matt. xxviii 18-20 among them. But I think such words were written down for Him because they seemed (in the opinion of the Evangelist) to be historically appropriate, not, first and foremost, because they were present-day watchwords of controversy.

In the first place it should be noticed that neither side is represented as appealing to words of Jesus. No doubt there was no authentic word of Jesus to appeal to, but the fact that we do not hear of any such words, genuine or forged, being quoted, suggests to me that these early Christians did not invent sayings of Christ so freely as seems to be assumed in some quarters. Further consideration shows also that the actually reported sayings would not have been so directly useful for controversial passages as might be thought at first sight.

"The Gospel must first be preached to all the Gentiles" (Mark xiii 10). This, as it stands, is a definite statement, a rather surprising one indeed to the historical critic. But even as it stands, without context, it would have been useless for controversial purposes between the "Judaizers" and the "Hellenists," for both were willing to make proselytes. The question was, upon what terms they might be admitted.[1] And when we look at the context of Mark xiii 10 we see that the subject is not missionary instruction, but warning that the Parusia may be delayed.

On the other hand the uncompromising severity of "Go not into the way of the Gentiles, and into any city of the Samaritans enter ye not; but go rather to the lost sheep of the House of Israel. . . . Amen I say to you, Ye will not have gone over the cities of Israel till the Son of Man be come" (Matt. x 5b, 6, 23) does demand the context to be considered. The words are given as an address to the Twelve early in the Gospel story: they are not the last final instructions of Jesus, though one passage corresponding to Mark xiii 9-13 is given in them (Matt. x 17-22), which is repeated in substance and partly in wording later on (Matt. xxiv 9-14). In the later passage, which corresponds in situation to Mark xiii 10, there is the definite statement that

---

[1] The writer of 1 Thess. ii 16 says indeed of the *Jews* (not the Jewish Christians), that they forbid to speak to the Gentiles that they may be saved, but this is a mere exaggeration.

the Gospel shall be proclaimed to the whole world. But where it is given in the early Galilean context this world-wide publication does not appear, only that the missioners will be brought before public tribunals "as a testimony to them and to the Gentiles." No doubt the discourse in Matt. x is a compilation, and therefore it does not quite hang together. But the Evangelist has at least attempted to keep to the Galilean situation: if he had not inserted vers. 17-22 (directly from Mark xiii, as I believe), we should not have doubted that the striking words I quoted above, which confine the ministry to the House of Israel, were what they profess to be, viz. instructions for the first Apostles in the early days in Galilee, when Jesus appears to have been expecting the End at once. Matt. x 23 is a strange saying, but if it was the invention of Jewish Christians about the time of the Conference at Jerusalem it is stranger still. It seems to me to testify to their unimaginative memory rather than to their powers of invention.

And the Message to be proclaimed, not only in the set of Sayings given in Matt. x, but also to the Seventy-Two according to Luke—what is it? That the Gentiles are fellow-heirs? Or that all proselytes must be circumcised, or must be baptized with such-and-such a formula? Nothing of the sort, as you know. The whole content of their "preaching," their proclamation, is "The Kingdom of God is at hand." This belongs historically to the earliest times, the times before the journey to Jerusalem and the Crucifixion. What a testimony to the general historicity of the methods, however unscientific, followed by all three Synoptic Evangelists!

I must add that I am not quite satisfied as to the punctuation of Mark xiii 9, 10, or in one small matter as to the text. It seems to me very likely that the original meaning is preserved in Matt x 18, i.e. that the disciples will be persecuted and arraigned by Jewish and even heathen authorities, and that this will be a testimony for them, as the Gospel must be proclaimed first, before the final catastrophe. The details must be left to a separate Note, but this seems to be the general view of the verse taken in early times.[1] With this interpretation the definite prophecy of heathen missions disappears, but it is easier to accept the words as a genuine reminiscence of the words of Jesus.

It is now time to bring these somewhat scattered observations upon Christian Beginnings to a close. I cannot help feeling that there will come a time in the not very distant future when the direct investigation of these early days of Christianity will have come to a standstill, when the task of rewriting the beginnings of the Christian Society will have been carried as far as the materials at our disposal will carry us. A great deal of the ancient presentation of the earliest Church History will have gone for ever, and on the other hand a number of new facts, some of great importance, will have emerged. It has been a wonderful century-and-a-half, since the beginnings of the historical criticism of the New Testament were laid by Semler and Herder and Reimarus and Lessing, and we are not yet at the end. But the process will not go on for ever, and this

[1] See the Note at the end.

for two reasons. The first is, of course, that the supply of fresh material is not likely to continue indefinitely: the East has been ransacked, and much of its treasures used. But there is a more potent reason still.

When Reimarus and Strauss were writing, the Bible itself was in a position of authority which it does not occupy to-day. The belief in the verbal inspiration of the Bible, by which was meant in practice its historical accuracy and its doctrinal homogeneity and infallibility, was very widely held. A new view of the Bible history then raised bitter opposition, often unfair opposition, and had to encounter great and deep-rooted prejudices. But it did excite interest, for in those days it was firmly believed that right views about the Bible mattered.

Well, we live in the New Age, we have shed most of our prejudices, we have lost our beliefs in the authority of the Past. The investigator of ancient history, including the Bible, has now a safer and easier task. He can investigate any period he likes without let or hindrance, and he runs little danger in publishing his conclusions. But alas, the old interest is dying. Too many people have come to believe that it doesn't matter; the unbelievers do not care to occupy themselves with these old tales now that their authority is discredited, and those who still believe in Religion tend more and more to rely on " Experience," on the experiences of Religion here and now. This is the case with Neo-Catholicism almost as much as with Methodism and other modern Protestant varieties of religion.

From the scientific, academical, point of view this means that Psychology gains and Historical Criticism loses. The bright, intelligent young man, whose interest in Religion has kept him from becoming an engineer or a geologist, now tends to take up the Philosophy of Religion with Psychology. Thirty years ago he would have occupied himself with the sort of subjects with which these Lectures have been concerned. In the next generation I fear there will be fewer investigators still who are occupied with the past.

Claudite iam riuos, pueri, sat prata biberunt: perhaps it will be better in the end for a fallow time to occur in the historical study of the New Testament. Much has been learnt in the last century; much of the old tradition has remained unshaken, for it was sound. No apocryphal work has been rediscovered that surpasses the Four Canonical Gospels, and of these Four the Gospel according to Mark has vindicated its position as a far more historical and intimate sketch of our Lord than anything that *a priori* was likely to have survived. In the ten Pauline Epistles (for I would include Ephesians) we have the thoughts, the emotions, the aspirations of the great Apostle of the Gentiles, forming at least a psychological document of extraordinary interest: he, being dead, yet speaketh. And finally in the Acts of the Apostles we have not a religious novel but an historical work. There are many details in these " Scenes from Early Days " that we cannot press, there are many and important gaps between the scenes. And undoubtedly there is in the way the story is told an idealizing, poetical element ;

the early part of Acts has in it something of the characteristics of a prose poem. But when we come to test it by the Letters of Paul we find it to be historical, not fabulous: it is a real guide to us, even for the earliest period.

NOTE ON THE TEXT AND INTERPRETATION OF MARK XIII 10

The text of Mark xiii 9ᵇ, 10, as printed by Westcott and Hort, is παραδώσουσιν ὑμᾶσ εἰσ συνέδρια καὶ εἰσ συναγωγὰσ δαρήσεσθε καὶ ἐπὶ ἡγεμόνων καὶ βασιλέων σταθήσεσθε ἕνεκεν ἐμοῦ εἰσ μαρτύριον αὐτοῖσ ¹⁰καὶ εἰσ πάντα τὰ ἔθνη πρῶτον δεῖ κηρυχθῆναι τὸ εὐαγγέλιον. Westcott and Hort of course insert a full-stop after αὐτοῖσ at the end of ver. 9: the remarkable thing is that almost all the early versions—Latin, Syriac, Sahidic—insert the stop after ἔθνη, and this punctuation is supported by Greek MSS. which insert δέ between πρῶτον and δεῖ.

The readings are:—πρωτον δει] אBDᵍʳ 28 *a n* vg, δει πρ. ⲋ A &c. *q* syr.hl, πρωτον δε δει W Θ 124 565, 108, 157

d c (k) ff i r vgᴸ ᵍ² (syr.S) arm sah.

(details of Latin evidence)
 . . . illis et in omnes gentes. *d ff k* (illos *k**) *i r*
 . . . illis et gentibus   *c*
 ad fin.] + omnibus gentibus *d ff tol g*²
        (+ εν πασιν τοις εθνεσιν Dᵍʳ)
 . . . . propter me at testimonium illos et in omnes gentes.
 set confortamini prius ‖ enim oportet praedicari euangelium *k*
 post in omn. gentes] + sed constantes estote *r tol g*²
   Note.—The colometry of D*d* favours *d* against D.

(details of Syriac evidence)
syr.S " . . . for witness to them and to all peoples; for first
     will this gospel be proclaimed."
syr.vg " . . . for their witness; but (δὲ) first is my gospel to
     be proclaimed in all peoples."

NOTE

The Gospel of Matthew appears to have used this passage twice over. A comparison of Matt. x 18 and Mark xiii 9 ("governors and kings") with Luke xii 11 makes it to me practically certain that "Matthew" has here deserted "Q" in order to adopt the wording of Mark xiii. When therefore "Matthew" comes to the Discourse on the Mount of Olives he is obliged to paraphrase Mark xiii 9-13, for the passage has been used already: the result is Matt. xxiv 9-14.

In the first case (Matt. x 18) Matthew agrees with the early translators of Mark. καὶ εἰσ πάντα τὰ ἔθνη is joined to what goes before; it is regarded as co-ordinate with αὐτοῖσ, and so Matthew writes it καὶ τοῖσ ἔθνεσιν. The rest of Mark xiii 10 is dropped altogether as inappropriate to the context.

In the second case (Matt. xxiv 14), on the other hand, Mark xiii 10^b is emphasized. Stress is laid on the idea that the End will not come till the Gospel has been proclaimed in all the world. But "all the Gentiles" are still grammatically connected with εἰσ μαρτύριον: both in Matt. x 18 and Matt. xxiv 14 we find εἰσ μαρτύριον ... τοῖσ ἔθνεσιν. Grammatically, therefore, the Gospel of Matthew in each case agrees with the construction of Mark xiii 9^b, 10, which takes εἰσ τὰ ἔθνη with εἰσ μαρτύριον and not with κηρυχθῆναι.

I cannot help feeling that the textual evidence, as in the somewhat similar case of Mark x. 29, 30, points to the original text of Mark having been here something rougher and less grammatical than that of our "best" authorities. The "best" text of Mark, viz. that of אB, seems to me that of an ancient MS. discovered and used by Origen. On the whole it is a very good text, far better than the current "Western" texts that it has supplanted. But here and there it has been emended, and in such cases traces of older readings are to be found in Western variants.

Here I feel inclined to accept the verdict of antiquity against that of grammar, and to suppose that Mark wrote εἰσ μαρτύριον αὐτοῖσ καὶ εἰσ τὰ ἔθνη, meaning εἰσ μαρτ. αὐτοῖσ καὶ τοῖσ ἔθνεσιν.

NOTE

The sense then will be: "These things *must* be, but the End is not yet. There will be troubles everywhere, as the Prophets have said. And don't think *you* will not suffer: you will be delated to the Beth Din, flogged in synagogues, have to stand your trial before Roman officials (ἡγεμόνων) and the Herods (βασιλέων), for my sake. So you will be a testimony to Jews and to Gentiles. This painful period of delay *must* be, so that the good news may be proclaimed."

Thus the mental horizon is still Palestine, not a formal worldwide evangelization. And consequently the historical critic may believe that the text, with its broken construction and Palestinian outlook, is really a reminiscence of words spoken by Jesus.

In Mark xiv 9 εἰσ ὅλον τὸν κόσμον only means "everywhere" in a general way; there is no direct anticipation of regular missions.

INDEX

Aelia, 61, 67, 69
Antioch, 52, 103, 130
Aramaic, 31, 33, 39f, 42 n, 44 n, 69, 75
Authority (of the Past), 6f, 141

Bar Cochba, 28
Barnabas, 101, 130
Beginnings of Christianity, 5, 11f
  quoted:
    i 102....18
      103....13
      303....92
      312.....57 n, 106 n
      314–18....135f
      319f....72
      320....74
      334....18
      362ff....30
      383....32, 36
    ii 171....76
      433....99 n
Benedictions, the Eighteen, 25 n
Bethune Baker, Dr., 26 n
Bousset, 49, 51
Bretschneider, 43

Caligula, 100
Christ, *see* Messiah
Clement of Rome, 38
Cornelius, 105, 115, 117

Damascus, 56
Decree, Apostolic, 112, 114f, 120f
Domine, quo vadis? 88

Eliezer b. Hyrḳanos, 73, 74f
Enoch, 30, 37, 65
Epiphanius, *Haer.* 30....62
Epistola Apostolorum, 89, 94
Eusebius:
  HE, ii 23....34 n, 57
  HE, iii 20....89 n
  HE, vii 19....67
Evangelion, 75

Father, Our, Jewish use, 25
Five Hundred, appearance to, *see* Pentecost
Five Thousand, feeding of, 76

Galilean Christianity, 84, 89f, 97
Gospel:
  according to Hebrews, 63, 75, 79
  according to Peter, 79, 94

Harnack, 133
Hegesippus, 57, 69
Hillel and Shammai, 73
Holy Men, 17, 61, 70

Jael, 45
James, "the Lord's Brother," 55f, 104
  his way of life, 58, 61, 70
  his abstinence, 62, 102
  martyrdom, 59
  grave, 60
  his chair, 67
  Christology, 64f, 71 n
  Epistle of James, 65–70
Jerome, 63, 72, 74

INDEX

Jesus:
  the Baptism, 22
  the Temptation, 23f
  "Son of God," 23ff, 29, 40
  "Son of Man," 30–5, 59, 64
  Lord, 44–8
  Messiah, 28
  Rabbi, 42f
  "Suffering Servant," 35ff, 39f
  His *Halacha*, 43
  His Words not invented, indiscriminately, 93f, 136f
Jewish Christianity, 63, 72
  concentrated at Jerusalem, 56, 76, 84, 89f, 132
  culture of, 73f, 133
  Evangelion, 75
  "Jezabel," 113f
Johanan b. Zakkai, 72f.
John the Baptist, 13–21
  not the Founder of a sect, 17 n
John, the Elder, 56
Josephus, 16, 18f
Journal of Theol. Studies:
  i 550....68
  xvii 296....88
Justin, *Ap*. I 66..49

Kaddish, 25 n
Kyrie, Kyrios, 46, 48f, 52

Lake, Prof., 115, 126

Mari, 45, 51
Messiah, Jewish, 27f, 71 n
Minim, 72, 74
Mishna, 73
Mithra, 49
Montefiore, C. G., 106
Moore, Prof. G. F., 12, 26, 72, 75
Mystery-Religions, 44, 49, 107

Naaman, 19, 45

Nazaraeans, 72f
New Birth, 108

Oblias, 58 n
Origen, 146
  in Joan., xix 23....67

Paul:
  his learning, 106, 109
  attitude to Law, 110
  attitude to the Decree, 120ff, 124
  his ordinances, 123
  his opponents at Corinth, 119
Philo, *in Flacc.* 6....45
Pentecost, 90f
"Places," the, 67
Pistis Sophia, 93

"Q," 15, 23, 38, 146

Rabbi, 42f, 44 n, 46
Rabbula, 66, 67 n
Rabbuni, 42, 45
Repentance, 16ff, 20
Resurrection:
  the Appearances:
    effect of, 46, 78
    where seen, 79–92
  Lucan accounts, 95f
Rhoda, 83
Ribboni, see Rabbuni
Rubil, 42 n

Saul, 106, 132
Schöttgen, 109 n
Scribes, 42
Ṣevi, Sabbatai, 27
Silas, Silvanus, 131ff
Sosthenes, 131
Stephen, 101f, 104, 133
"Strangled" food, 114, 125

Taurobolium, 108
Tertius, 131
Testamentum Domini, 94

Thackeray, Dr. H. St. J., 107
Timothy, 131
Tithe, 63
Titus, 57, 118
Turner, Prof. C. H., 68

Vegetarianism, 62, 102, 116, 121

Weiss, J., 76
Wrede, 26

BIBLICAL REFERENCES

2 KINGS (4 REGN.)

v 13	45
14	19

ISAIAH

iii 10	60 n
v 9	66
viii 14	72
xlii 1, etc.	41
liii 1	38
10*b*, 11*b*	37 n
12	37

DANIEL

iv 16	45 n

ZECHARIAH

xiii 7	81

MATTHEW

ii 1	16 n
iii 1f	15
13	16 n
iv 12	24
17	16
viii 17	37
x 5f	137
17–22	137f
18	139, 146
23	137f
xiv 12	17 n
xxi 21	44
30	46
xxiv 14	137, 146
xxv 31ff	37
xxvii 63	45 n

xxviii 9–20	83
16	80
18–20	135

MARK

i 4	20
14	24
15	16
ii 18	17 n
27f	33
vii 9, 18	43
viii 13–21	77
29	28
36	31 n
ix 9–13	33f
x 29f	146
45	29, 37 n
51	42
xiii 9, 10	136ff, 145ff
14	100
32	96
35ff	35
xiv 9	147
14	46
25, 42	88
28	81, 89
xvi 7	81
8	80, 83

LUKE

iii 7–14	15, 21
iv 43	16
xii 11	146
xiii 24ff	65 n
xvi 16	16
xvii 20	96

xviii 31	. . .	95
xxi 36 .	. . .	35 n
xxii 37	. . .	37
xxiv 34	. . .	47
38f, 49	. . .	95

JOHN

i 12	. . .	48
32–34	. . .	22
41, 49	. . .	27
iii 5 ff	. . .	108
iv 25f	. . .	27
viii 32, 34	. . .	48
x 24	. . .	27
xi 2	. . .	48
xii 21	. . .	46
38	. . .	38
xiii 13	. . .	44
xv 15	. . .	48
xx 15	. . .	46
16	. . .	42
19ff, 26ff	. . .	81
28	. . .	48
xxi 14	. . .	81
23	. . .	82

ACTS

i 7	. . .	95
ii 36	. . .	47
vi 14	. . .	101
vii 56	. . .	34, 35 n
viii 32f	. . .	38
x 42	. . .	30
xi 3	. . .	115
19ff	. . .	103
30	. . .	57, 117f
xii 3	. . .	103
17, 19	. . .	104
23	. . .	99
xv 22, 32	. . .	132
28	. . .	113
xvii 31	. . .	30
xix 3	. . .	17 n
xxi 24	. . .	102

ROMANS

i–xiv	. . .	126
i 7, 15	. . .	126
ix–xi	. . .	130
x 9	. . .	44
16	. . .	38
xiv 20f	. . .	116
22	. . .	128
23	. . .	127
xv 1–13	. . .	127
19–29	.	56, 125, 127
xvi 1	. . .	127
22	. . .	131
25–27	. . .	126

1 CORINTHIANS

v, vi 12ff, vii	. .	120
vi 15	. . .	122
vii 18f	. . .	119
viii	.	120, 124, 128
x 19–32	. . .	120
27	. . .	125
xi 4, 14	. . .	123
xii 3	. . .	44, 48
xv 3–8	. .	79, 90f
25ff, 51ff	. . .	130
xvi 21	. .	133 n

2 CORINTHIANS

iv, v	. . .	126
vii 9, 10	. . .	20
xi 32	. . .	56

GALATIANS

i 16ff	. . .	55
22	. . .	56
ii 1–10	. . .	117f
3–5	. . .	118
8	. . .	117
12	. . .	56, 115
vi 15	. . .	109

Ephesians

iv 8f	107 n
vi 21	131

Colossians

ii 23	123 n
iv 18	133 n

1 Thessalonians

i 9, 10	130
ii 14–16	130
14	56
16	137 n
18	132
iii 1, 6	128
iv 2f	129

2 Thessalonians

ii 3, 7	130
iii 17	132

Hebrews

ix 28	37

James

i 1, ii 1	71 n
ii 2ff	69
iii 6	69
iv 1	69
v 4	66, 69

1 Peter

i 23, etc.	108
ii 22ff	37

Jude

1	48

Revelation

i 13	35 n
ii 20	114
24	113
v 6	38 n
xiii 8	38 n
xiv 5	38 n
14	35 n